BLENHEIM
Landscape for a Palace
SECOND EDITION

EDITED BY

James Bond & Kate Tiller

FOREWORD BY HIS GRACE THE DUKE OF MARLBOROUGH

SUTTON PUBLISHING

OXFORD UNIVERSITY DEPARTMENT FOR CONTINUING EDUCATION

First published in 1987 by Alan Sutton Publishing Limited, an imprint of
Sutton Publishing Limited · Phoenix Mill · Thrupp · Stroud · Gloucestershire · GL5 2BU
in association with Oxford University Department for Continuing Education

This revised edition published in 1997 by Sutton Publishing Limited

British Library Cataloguing in Publication Data

Blenheim: landscape for a palace.
    1. Blenheim Park (England) — History – 87
    I. Tiller, Kate II. Bond, James, *1944–*
    942.5'71   SB466.G8B5

ISBN 0-7509-1589-7

Acknowledgements: The editors are grateful to the Duke of Marlborough, Mr R. Cobham, Mr P. Everett and
Dr G.P. Thomas for their help and support during the preparation of both editions of this book.

Picture Credits: Permission to use the following illustrations is gratefully acknowledged:

Illustrations 52, 61, 64, 66, 70, 82, 83, 84, 86, 89, 90, 91, 100, 114 by kind permission of His Grace the Duke
of Marlborough; frontispiece, 28, 29, 67, 75, 85, 88, 95, 96, 105, 107, 108, 109, 113, 115, 116, 118 Oxfordshire
County Libraries; 1, 51, 76, 97 Aerofilms Ltd; 3, 53, 54 National Portrait Gallery; 10, 13, 79 Ashmolean
Museum, Oxford; 45, 71 Oxfordshire County Council; 32, 34, 68 The British Library; 8 Oxfordshire
Architectural and Historical Society, D.B. Harden and the late C. Musgrave; 55, 63, 65, 81, 106 The Bodleian
Library, Oxford; 80 D. McQuilty of Colvin & Moggridge; 97, 98 Colvin & Moggridge; 121 *Oxford Mail and
Times*; 122, 123, 125, 126, 127, 128, 129 Ralph Cobham; 130, 131 Paul Hutton; 92 Woodstock Borough
Council; other photographs, maps and plans C.J. Bond.

Maps and plans by H. Moggridge and R. Cobham in chapters 8 and 10 have previously appeared in articles by the
authors in *Landscape Design*, *Landscape Research* and the *Journal of the Arboriculture Association*, as cited in those
chapters.

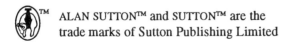

Typesetting and origination by
Sutton Publishing Limited.
Printed in Great Britain by
Butler & Tanner, Frome, Somerset.

Entering Blenheim Park:
The Triumphal Arch from
the north, *c.* 1930

CONTENTS

LIST OF CONTRIBUTORS

JAMES BOND, B.A., F.S.A., M.I.F.A., was born in Oxford and has known Blenheim Park all his life. Trained as an historical geographer at the University of Birmingham, he undertook a survey of Woodstock and Blenheim for his undergraduate dissertation in 1966. On returning to Oxfordshire in 1974 as Assistant Field Officer in the County Council's Department of Museum Services he became based at Woodstock, where his work with the County Sites and Monuments Record enabled him to resume his interest in the history and archaeology of the park. He left the Oxfordshire Museum Service in 1986 and now lives near Bristol, where he works freelance, lecturing and writing on landscape history.

JOHN CAMPBELL, A.M.A., was born in west Oxfordshire and has spent most of his life there. He studied at London University, and after teaching in various schools joined Oxfordshire County Council's Department of Museum Services in 1974, where he is responsible for natural history within the Environmental Record Section. For ten years he was editor of the County Bird Report. He has had a long-term interest in the natural history of Blenheim.

RALPH COBHAM, B.A., Agr.B., Dip.Agric.Econ., M.Sc., F.L.I., M.I.L.A.M., spent part of his formative years in the landscape setting designed for Stowe by Capability Brown. Throughout his subsequent career, both in Southern Ireland and in England, he has been fortunate to live and work in many historic parkland landscapes. Since 1972 he has been in private practice as a Land Use and Landscape Management Adviser and was until 1996 the Senior Partner of Cobham Resource Consultants, now Scott Wilson Resource Consultants with one of its UK offices in Oxfordshire. In 1981 his firm was one of two jointly appointed to prepare a restoration plan for the Blenheim parklands. He lectures widely both in the U.K. and abroad on creative aspects of estate management.

PHILIP EVERETT, F.R.I.C.S., has been Land Agent to the Blenheim estate since 1986, and has been centrally involved in the implementation and development of the Landscape Restoration and Management Plan for Blenheim Park.

DAVID GREEN, F.S.A., lived in Oxfordshire from 1943 to his death in 1985. During these years he studied and became an authority on Blenheim and the Marlborough family, in particular on the contribution of Capability Brown to the Blenheim landscape. He wrote many books, including the standard history of Blenheim Palace, published in 1951, the biographies of Queen Anne and Sarah, Duchess of Marlborough, and the official Guide Books to Blenheim Palace and to its park and gardens. He delivered a memorable paper at the 1983 symposium on Blenheim, but sadly did not live to see his contribution into print.

PAUL HUTTON, F.R.I.C.S., a partner in the firm of Smiths Gore, Chartered Surveyors, spent the major part of his professional career as a Resident Land Agent on large estates. After thirteen years in North Yorkshire, he moved south to take over the management of the Blenheim Estate, including Blenheim Palace and the Park, in 1978. Shortly thereafter, following the ravages of Dutch Elm Disease and the loss of many of the mature beeches in Blenheim Park, he played a leading role in the preparation of the long-term Restoration Plan for this historic landscape.

HAL MOGGRIDGE, O.B.E., P.P.L.I., R.I.B.A., A.A.dip., trained as an architect at the Architectural Association before becoming a landscape architect. He worked with Sir Geoffrey Jellicoe, then in Ghana, then in the G.L.C. Town Development Division, before entering private practice. In 1969 he moved to Oxfordshire to enter partnership with the late Brenda Colvin and has continued as principal of the landscape practice Colvin & Moggridge. Early in 1981 he was commissioned with Ralph Cobham to prepare a Landscape Restoration Plan for Blenheim and continues, on an annual basis, to be involved in the formulation and implementation of both strategic and detailed restoration work in the Park.

DOROTHY STROUD, M.B.E., F.S.A., Hon.F.R.I.B.A., was born in London in 1910. After several years on the staff of *Country Life* she joined the National Buildings Record (now part of the National Monuments Record) on its inception in 1941. In 1946 she was appointed Assistant Curator of Sir John Soane's Museum, from which she retired in 1984. Since 1982 she has been a Vice President of the Garden History Society. Her publications include biographies of 'Capability' Brown, Henry Holland, George Dance and Sir John Soane.

KATE TILLER, B.A., Ph.D., F.S.A., F.R.Hist.S., is University Lecturer in Local History at Oxford University Department for Continuing Education and Fellow of Kellogg College. She organised the original conference at Blenheim Palace marking the bicentenary of Capability Brown, upon the proceedings of which this book is based. Dr Tiller has been responsible for introducing Undergraduate Certificate, and postgraduate Master's and Doctoral programmes in local history at Oxford. She has written widely on local history, including a number of Oxfordshire studies, and takes a particular interest in garden and landscape history, working regularly in collaboration with the Garden History Society.

Blenheim Palace.

FOREWORD
by His Grace the Duke of Marlborough

I am delighted to welcome the publication of this revised and updated edition of *Blenheim: Landscape for a Palace*. When the first edition appeared, in 1987, I noted in my Foreword that, whilst Blenheim Palace had attracted intense interest from many writers over the years, the great park surrounding it had been less fully appreciated. Now, in 1996, Blenheim's designation as a World Heritage Site is firmly established and rests not only on its outstanding architecture and the national and international historical roles of my ancestor the first Duke and Sir Winston Churchill, but also on a recognition of its associated landscape as one of the most internationally famous works of landscape art.

Blenheim Park is rich in historical associations, including medieval and Tudor monarchs and, since 1704, my own family. As a historical landscape the Park is a striking example of how long centuries of use and development have left fascinating layers of visual evidence which, with the help of the contributors to this volume, can now be understood and enjoyed afresh. The Park illustrates the work of great figures in English landscape gardening, especially Capability Brown, in celebration of whose bicentenary these papers were first given, in the New Restaurant at Blenheim. However, there is much more – from prehistoric earthworks and Roman remains to the new features added to Brown's eighteenth-century landscape by my predecessors in the nineteenth and early years of the present century.

Now I have the task of preserving and enhancing this rich and varied legacy. I am particularly glad to see the attention paid in this book to Blenheim Park present as well as past, for current developments at Blenheim surely present a striking case study of the issues of conservation, of management, of balancing the old and new, encountered by so many concerned with historic landscapes and gardens in Britain.

When the conference, from which this book stems, was held in 1983 the master plan for the restoration and management of the landscape of Blenheim Park was in the very early stages of implementation. It has been a remarkable undertaking, seeking to accommodate the needs of agriculture, fishing, game, nature conservation, historical preservation and public access.

In 1996 we can take stock of the first phase of that plan and look forward to a second fifteen-year agenda for action, taking us into the new millennium. This new edition of *Blenheim: Landscape for a Palace* brings the story up to date and also incorporates the findings of historical research undertaken since 1987. The latest chapter in the long history of Blenheim Park will, I hope, add interest to the fascinating earlier history also recounted here and assure all of us who so much enjoy and appreciate this outstanding piece of English landscape, of its continuing future.

Marlborough

EDITORIAL NOTE

The origins of this volume lie in a day school organised by Dr Kate Tiller under the auspices of the then Department for External Studies of Oxford University. The original conference was held in association with the Garden History Society at the Riding School at Blenheim Palace, by permission of His Grace the Duke of Marlborough, on 21 May 1983. The event commemorated the bicentenary of the death of 'Capability' Brown, the famous landscape gardener who did so much splendid work at Blenheim. During the course of the day, Brown's contribution was examined in considerable depth; but in addition, the evolution of the Blenheim landscape both before and after Brown was explored, from its beginnings in prehistory through to the management problems of the present day and, indeed, the prospects for the future. In view of the immense importance of Blenheim in the history of English parks and gardens, it was felt that the proceedings warranted publication, and so each of the talks was tape-recorded.

In preparing transcripts of these tape-recordings for publication, some modifications were made in order to reduce overlap and duplication. Bibliographies and footnote references were introduced, in order to provide a guide for those wishing to follow up the sources. Most papers given at the day school were accompanied by colour slides, but it proved impossible to reproduce all the illustrations, although it is hoped that no important information has been sacrificed. Sections of some of the original lectures were reorganised in order to achieve a more coherent chronological structure to the volume. In taking these necessary editorial liberties, we hope that the views and intentions of all the speakers have been safeguarded and that something of the flavour and character of each individual contribution is preserved. In order to give substance to an aspect touched upon in several other papers, an additional chapter on the natural history of Blenheim was added.

Since *Blenheim: Landscape for a Palace* first appeared in 1987, a number of significant developments in both historical knowledge of the Park and in its restoration and management have taken place. In particular, Alan Crossley's account of Blenheim, published in the *Victoria History of the County of Oxford*, volume XII, in 1990, and the completion in 1996 of the first phase of the landscape restoration and management plan for the Park, are reflected in revisions to chapters 4 and 5 and in a new chapter 12. Whilst the bulk of the original material still stands we welcome this opportunity, with the 1987 edition out of print, to bring the story up to date. We would like to thank all the contributors for their help, patience and forbearance in the preparation of each edition of this book.

James Bond
Walton-in-Gordano, Somerset, 1997

Kate Tiller
Rewley House, Oxford, 1997

1. INTRODUCTION

Dorothy Stroud

1. Blenheim Park and Palace from the south.

THE ARTICLES contained in this volume are based upon papers delivered at a symposium arranged by the Oxford University Department for External Studies and held at Blenheim Palace on 21 May 1983. 1983 was the bicentenary of the death of Lancelot 'Capability' Brown, the central figure in the history of British landscape gardening. Blenheim is surely the most outstanding of all Brown's works, and it was a happy inspiration to hold the symposium in such a splendid venue. The tribute which these proceedings pay to Brown as the creator of so many landscape gardens and not a few houses is long overdue. In his own day, his achievements were widely recognised and appreciated; but, as one of his obituarists foretold at his death in 1783, such was the effect of his genius that, where he was the happiest man, he would be least remembered, so closely did he copy nature that his works would be mistaken. That is, indeed, precisely what happened; and, all too often, succeeding generations of owners, whilst proud of their parks and the wealth of fine trees, lawns and lakes with which these were adorned, regarded them as a fortunate dispensation of nature, while Brown's genius and the expenditure and patience of their forefathers was forgotten. On the rare occasions when Brown's name appears in nineteenth-century writings, it is usually to comment on his odd nickname of 'Capability', or to denigrate

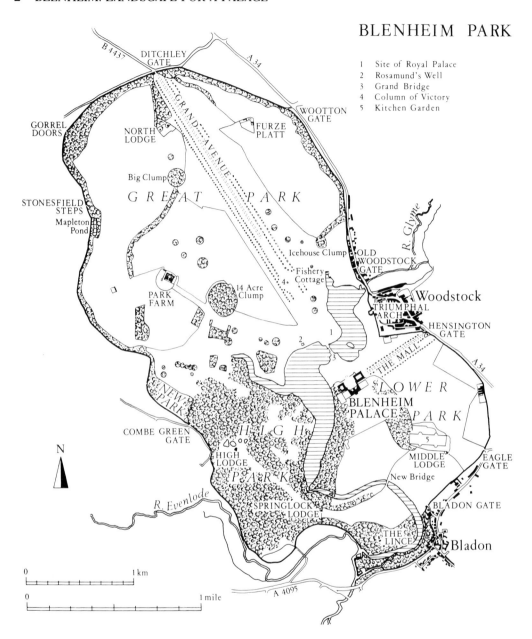

BLENHEIM PARK

1   Site of Royal Palace
2   Rosamund's Well
3   Grand Bridge
4   Column of Victory
5   Kitchen Garden

2.   Blenheim Park: major features.

him as the arch-destroyer of parterres and avenues. This is quite unjust, but unfortunately this hostile attitude to Brown and to landscape gardeners in general persisted until the early 1930s. Then, largely due to a series of articles in *Country Life* and elsewhere by that fine scholar and keen amateur gardener, the late Christopher Hussey, the value of Brown's contribution began to be recognised.

I say 'began to be recognised', because when I ventured to start collecting material on Brown in 1939 and then resumed my researches at the end of the War, there was still a fairly strong antipathy to Brown and the landscape school. 'Madam', replied the owner of what is now proudly advertised as one of Brown's finest parks, 'we have no drawings or papers relating to Capability Brown; he carried out some work here, but we have no reason to be grateful to him.' Another testy owner of a famous Yorkshire landscape garden admitted grudgingly that, although he had no wealth of documents, his grounds did show signs of the nefarious ideas of 'Capability' and his like. A few owners, though well enough disposed, were merely ignorant: such as the one who assured me that 'Brown did no work at all in these grounds', and then, fifteen years after I had written my book, wrote delightedly to tell me that 'three Capability Brown plans about five feet square had suddenly come to light.' One wonders where they had been lurking all that time.

3.   Lancelot 'Capability' Brown: Portrait by Nathaniel Dance.

Today we have seen the wheel come full circle. We are now sufficiently far removed in time to appreciate garden history and physical examples of it which have survived, irrespective of century or fashion. There is now no question as to the immense value of the eighteenth-century landscape – but what of its future? Gardens and parks have now found a place in the provisions of the National Heritage Act, which means that those designated as being of national importance may receive qualification for tax exemption or even, possibly, financial aid. For the landscape, this will require a great deal of expertise in large-scale restoration and maintenance. The project in hand here at Blenheim promises to set a fine example, and I am sure that it will stimulate interest in the restoration and maintenance of gardens elsewhere. For this reason, I welcome with great interest this account of Blenheim Park, both before and after the work of Capability Brown, and the light it throws upon the present-day appreciation of this outstanding piece of landscape heritage and the strategies for maintaining it for the enjoyment of future generations.

2. BLENHEIM: THE GEOGRAPHICAL SETTING

James Bond

BLENHEIM PARK is situated some 12km (*c.* 8 miles) to the north-north-west of Oxford, immediately adjoining the small town of Woodstock. The main A34 Oxford–Woodstock–Chipping Norton–Stratford-on-Avon road skirts its eastern side for a distance of 3km (just under 2 miles). To the south-east the park abuts the A4095 Witney road as it passes through the village of Bladon. To the north the Ditchley Gate of the park leads out onto the B4437 road to Charlbury close to the point where this is joined by a minor road to Stonesfield, which is followed by the park wall for some 600m (*c.* 650 yards). To the west the park faces open country, overlooking the village of Combe, with fragments of the ancient Forest of Wychwood, of which it once formed a part, clothing the more distant horizons.

Blenheim lies at the foot of the dip-slope of the Cotswold escarpment, near the point where the hills level out into the flat lands of the Upper Thames valley. Its relief is varied, without ever being extreme. It is drained by the small River Glyme, which passes through it from north to south, dividing it into two unequal parts; the damming of this river in the eighteenth century formed the great lake which is the centrepiece of the landscaping. Below the Lince Bridge at the southern extremity of the park the Glyme falls into one of the principal north-bank tributaries of the Thames, the River Evenlode, which is itself followed by the park boundary for some 2km (*c.* 2,200 yards). This stretch of the Evenlode, from the vicinity of Stonesfield down to Bladon, is a classic example of a misfit stream, where the diminutive volume of the present river is totally out of scale with the majestic sweep of the valley meanders. The meanders must have been formed on a near-level clay or clay-intercalated surface by a much larger mature river during the Pleistocene period, becoming incised when the drainage was superimposed over the limestone dip-slope.[1] Various explanations have been put forward to account for these anomalies, including the curtailment of a large consequent river, which in the Miocene or Pliocene period may have flowed across the cover-rocks over the Cotswolds from the Welsh hills; the smaller-scale river-capture of the headwaters of the Evenlode by streams feeding the Stour and draining ultimately into the Severn; the erosive effect of glacial meltwaters pouring down from ice-sheets clothing the Midlands, or of spring floodwaters following the melting of the heavy winter snows precipitated in periglacial conditions; recent reduction of rainfall; and the absorption of much of the surface run-off by alluvial deposits following the aggradation of the

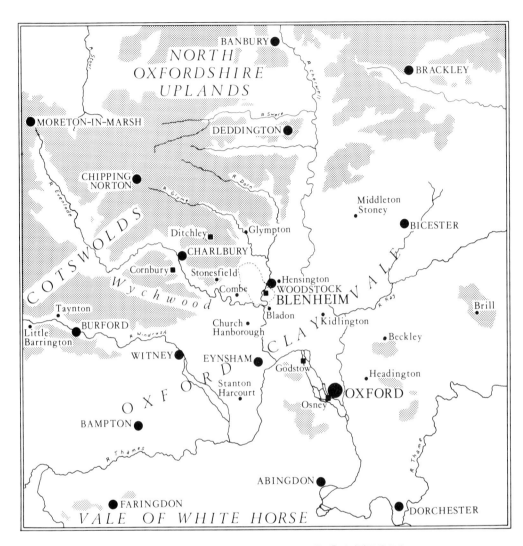

BLENHEIM PARK: LOCATION

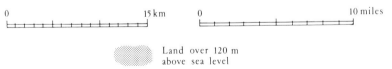

Land over 120 m
above sea level

4.   Blenheim Park: location.

valley resulting from an increase of load relative to stream volume.[2] Whatever the causes, the lowest reaches of the Glyme were clearly affected by the same processes, for below the cascade forming the exit from the lake the river swings in a spectacular incised meander around the Lince, travelling some 2.5km (*c.* 2,650 yards) round to the Evenlode confluence, but leaving an isthmus only 250m (*c.* 280 yards) wide at the Springlock Lodge.

The smaller portion of Blenheim Park, the Lower Park east of the Glyme, is an area of fairly subdued relief, reaching its greatest elevation of 96m (*c.* 315 feet) O.D. in the vicinity of Blenheim Palace itself, and falling gently away south-eastwards to about 76m (*c.* 250 feet) by the boundary wall against Bladon village. On the western side, however, the plateau terminates in a quite sharp edge, dropping into the Glyme valley. The slopes are steepest, achieving gradients of about 1 in 4, immediately west and immediately north of Blenheim Palace, though this effect may be exaggerated by the massive earth-moving carried out to create the lake in the eighteenth century.

West of the Glyme the larger portion of the park is itself subdivided into several distinct blocks. The lowest of these is the peninsula between the Springlock Lodge and the Lince, already mentioned. To the north-west the High Park occupies an area of rising ground, which reaches its maximum elevation at 116m (*c.* 380 feet) near High Lodge. The High Park is delimited on the north by a narrow, steep-sided dry valley, which separates it from the Great Park to the north. The head of this valley lies just outside the Gorrel Doors at the north-west corner of Blenheim, and the western wall of the Great Park follows the valley bottom, which initially is comparatively shallow and open, past the Stonesfield Steps and Mapleton Pond. Near the point where the park wall diverges, climbing up the southern flank towards the New Park, the valley becomes steeper and more constricted, and it is penetrated by a long, sinuous arm of the lake.

The main part of the Great Park is a wide, open, windswept plateau, rising to 111m (364 feet) above sea level. Towards its eastern margins it is again cut by another dry valley above the Fishery Cottage, the head of which bifurcates near the Icehouse Clump, one arm forming the shallow combe north of the Column of Victory, the other, longer arm curving round from the east, with its ultimate source above Furze Platt. The origin of these dry valleys, like others on the Cotswolds, is likely to have occurred in nival regimes during the Pleistocene period.[3] The character of all the dry valleys west of the Glyme, open and

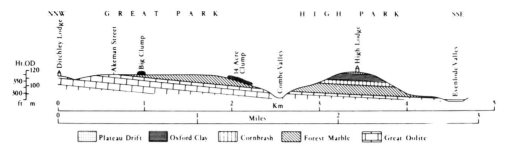

BLENHEIM PARK :   Generalised Geological Section, NNW-SSE

5. Blenheim Park: the geological make-up.

shallow at the head, becoming deeply incised lower down, indicates that the streams which once flowed down them were affected by the same processes of rejuvenation and incision that affected the Glyme and Evenlode.

Geologically[4] the oldest rocks within the park are the Great Oolite series of the Middle Jurassic, which form the basis for much of the Great Park to the north. Elsewhere the Great Oolite contains some important building stones, notably the Taynton limestones, and a lens of fissile, calcareous sandstone outcropping around Stonesfield, which was formerly mined for stone roofing-slates. In the park the so-called White Limestone, creamy marly limestones interspersed with hard white bands and layers of green and brown clays and marls, is predominant.

Above this is the Forest Marble, a flaggy oolite with occasional bands of blue-grey and white clay, which forms a capping over the White Limestone in the highest part of the Great Park between Park Farm and Grim's Ditch. The Kemble Beds, comprising the lowest part of the Forest Marble, locally consist of a blue clay, which appears in the south-eastern half of the Lower Park between the Home Farm, the Cowyards and the Kitchen-Garden, and in the Lince peninsula. Narrow bands of Forest Marble also outcrop along the valley sides along the edge of the Great Park north of Old Woodstock, east of the Glyme immediately below the Palace, north of High Lodge, and on Dog Kennel Hill, overlooking the Evenlode.

The Forest Marble is succeeded by the Lower Cornbrash, a shelly, hard, rubbly limestone which makes a very limited appearance on the eastern margins near the Old Woodstock Gate and on the slopes north, east and south of High Lodge. It has a more extensive outcrop east of the Glyme, where it underlies part of the north-western part of the Lower Park plateau, including the Hensington Gate and the Temple of Flora.

Parts of the northern half of the park are pockmarked with small abandoned quarries where the various Jurassic limestones have been explored. The largest is that in the Icehouse Clump, where the old working face exposed 2.4m (8 feet) of Cornbrash resting on 3m (10 feet) of Forest Marble.[5] John Vanbrugh, architect of Blenheim Palace, reported to the Duke of Marlborough four days after the foundation stone was laid, 'We have Open'd four or five Quarrys in the Park which afford Stone for Inside Walls ... but there is only One where we find any freestone, and little of that fitt to Stand without doors, tho' very usefull in many places within.'[6] The failure of the quarries in the park to produce freestone of any quality led to a search being made over a wider area, and supplies were secured first from Glympton and Cornbury, and subsequently from Burford, Taynton, Little Barrington, Sherborne, Bourton-on-the-Hill, Heythrop, Headington and other localities.[7] Arkell's examinations of the facing-stone of the palace led him to conclude that much of the visible material came from the top layers of the Clypeus Grit within the Inferior Oolite, which, taken alongside the documentary evidence, makes the Buckleap Quarry at Cornbury the most likely source.[8] The fine-grained water-marked oolite used in the rusticated masonry of the corner blocks is probably from Taynton.[9]

Geologically the youngest of the solid deposits found within the park is the Oxford Clay of the Upper Jurassic, which in effect forms a discontinuous minor scarp between Combe and Bladon Heath. An outlier of Oxford Clay, detached from the main outcrop by the Evenlode valley, forms the summit of the most elevated part of the park around High Lodge.

The superficial deposits include a small, thin patch of unbedded yellowish-brown clayey gravel, the Plateau Drift, which caps the Oxford Clay outcrop between High Lodge and the Combe Gate. The most distinctive characteristic of this deposit is the preponderance of Bunter and Lickey Quartzite pebbles brought down from the Birmingham area with other erratic materials. It is generally ungraded and unstratified, marked by sudden changes of facies, and some of the pebbles display parallel striations. The origins of the Plateau Drift are still somewhat controversial. Sandford[10] initially regarded it as a marine deposit, brought by dirt-laden ice rafts floating in a high-level Pleistocene sea. Arkell[11] believed the Northern Drift plateau deposits around Combe and Blenheim to be of fluviatile origin, the remains of a deltaic deposit laid down by the progenitor of the Evenlode, swollen by outwash from the retreating ice-sheets, at the point where it emerged from the

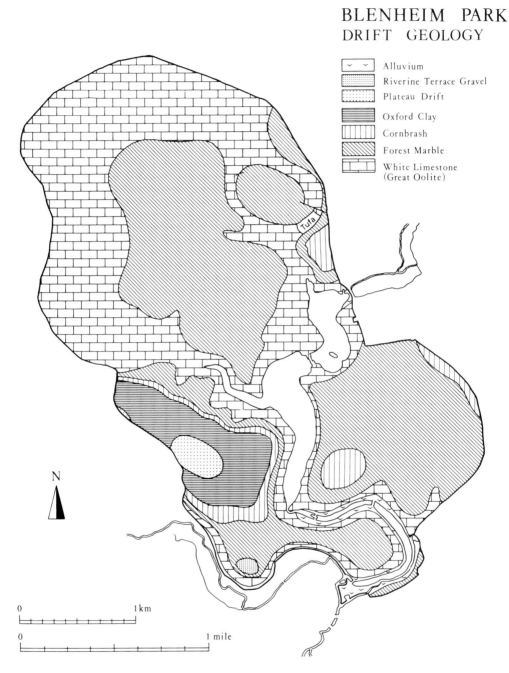

BLENHEIM PARK
DRIFT GEOLOGY

Alluvium
Riverine Terrace Gravel
Plateau Drift
Oxford Clay
Cornbrash
Forest Marble
White Limestone
(Great Oolite)

N

0   1 km

0   1 mile

6. Blenheim Park: drift geology.

Cotswold dip-slope out onto the Oxford Clay vale. A third possibility is that the deposit is of purely glacial origin, having been laid down under a decaying lobe of ice spilling over from the Midlands through the Moreton Gap into the Evenlode valley, probably during the Berrocian (Gunz) glaciation. Recently the glacial and fluvio-glacial theory has been the preferred one.[12] This drift capping over the Oxford Clay provides a small perched water-table, which accounts for the rather damp character of the High Lodge area. Lower down, within the convex lobe of the Evenlode valley south-west of the Springlock Lodge is a small patch of riverine gravel containing oolitic pebbles and sand, which appears to be a fragment of the Wolvercote Terrace, the second-highest and second-oldest of the four main Thames terraces, now attributed to the later Wolstonian glacial period.[13] Alluvium floors the narrow flood-plains of the Evenlode and Glyme.

North of the Icehouse Clump, seepages issuing from the Great Oolite aquifer at a time when the water-table was higher have partly choked the dry valley with deposits of tufa, which form a series of swells or steps in the valley floor.

The soils of the Great Oolite are generally shallow rendzinas, varying from a brash with angular limestone lumps to a friable red-brown loam. These soils have traditionally been regarded as favourable for cereal cultivation, and since the nineteenth century arable farming has indeed spread over much of the Great Park. The Cornbrash soils are variable, light, reddish-brown stonebrashes, which tend to be more difficult to work in wet weather, and form clods which dry hard. The Oxford Clay gives a cold, stiff, brownish-grey soil, sticky and tenacious when wet and drying into hard, tough clods; the parts of the park where it occurs have remained under wood-pasture dominated by pedunculate oak.

The geology and geomorphology of the area provides a stage upon which man has at various times carried out a range of activities. While it is necessary to have some understanding of the ways in which physiographic factors have shaped the stage, however, it would be wrong to relate human activity to the physical landscape in a deterministic way. Central Oxfordshire is an area without extremes and without insuperable natural constraints. The area has been occupied by man for many thousands of years, and it is the technological, cultural and historical background which has been the most significant influence upon the landscape, factors which will be examined in subsequent chapters.

References

1   The classic paper on this subject is DAVIS W.M. 1899: 'The Drainage of Cuestas', *Proceedings of the Geologists' Association* Vol. 16, pp. 87–93, which discusses the Evenlode gorge as one of its examples. See also ARKELL W.J. 1947: 'The Geology of the Evenlode Gorge', *Proceedings of the Geologists' Association* Vol. 58, pp. 87–114.

2   Some of these theories are discussed by BECKIT H.O. 1926: 'Physiography of the Oxford Region' in WALKER J.J. (Ed.), *The Natural History of the Oxford District*, pp. 1–20.

3   *Cf.* BECKINSALE R.P. 1970: 'Physical Problems of Cotswold Rivers and Valleys', *Proceedings of Cotteswold Naturalists' Field Club* Vol. 35, pp. 194–205.

4   The first detailed description of the local geology is by HULL E. 1859: *The Geology of the Country around Woodstock, Oxfordshire*, the Geological Survey memoir prepared to accompany the first geological mapping of the area (Old Series, Sheet 45 SW, 1859). The following section is based largely upon ARKELL W.J. 1947: *The Geology of Oxford* (Clarendon Press, Oxford); and upon RICHARDSON L., ARKELL W.J. & DINES H.G. 1946: *Geology of the Country around Witney* (Memoirs of the Geological Survey of England and Wales, HMSO, London), prepared as a commentary upon the Geological Survey Sheet 236 (Witney), Drift edition (1938).

5   First described by HULL E. (*op. cit.*), p. 24.

6   Blenheim Muniments A–I–27, quoted in GREEN D. 1951: *Blenheim Palace* (Country Life, London), pp. 56–7.

7   GREEN D. (*op. cit.*), pp. 56–61.

8   ARKELL W.J. 1948: 'The Building-Stones of Blenheim Palace, Cornbury Park, Glympton Park and Heythrop House, Oxfordshire', *Oxoniensia* Vol. 13, pp. 49–54.

9   ARKELL W.J. 1951: 'Building-Stones of Blenheim Palace,' *Oxoniensia*, Vol. 16, pp. 88–9.

10 SANDFORD K.S. 1924: 'River Gravels of the Oxford District', *Quarterly Jnl. of Geological Soc.* Vol. 80, p. 113; and 1929: 'The Erratic Blocks and the Age of the Southern Limit of Glaciation in the Oxford District', *Quarterly Jnl. of Geological Soc.* Vol. 85, pp. 359–388.

11 ARKELL W.J. 1947: *Geology of Oxford*, pp. 191–201.

12 GOUDIE A.S. & HART M.G. 1975: 'Pleistocene Events and Forms in the Oxford Region' in SMITH C.G. & SCARGILL D.I. (Eds.), *Oxford and its Region: Geographical Essays* (Oxford University Press), pp. 3–13, esp. 5–6.

13 BRIGGS D.J. & GILBERTSON D.D. 1974: 'Recent Studies of Pleistocene Deposits in the Evenlode Valley and adjacent areas of the Cotswolds', *Sound (Jnl. of Plymouth Polytechnic Geo-Society)* Vol. 3, pp. 7–22; GOUDIE & HART (*op. cit.*), p. 7.

3. THE PARK BEFORE THE PALACE: ARCHAEOLOGY AND LANDSCAPE

James Bond

Introduction

THE SCENE which confronts present-day visitors to Blenheim who enter the park from the direction of Woodstock is predominantly a contrived landscape designed in the eighteenth century, dominated on the one hand by the early eighteenth-century architectural contribution of Sir John Vanbrugh – the Palace itself and the Grand Bridge – and on the other hand by the magnificent lake and plantations of trees contributed by Lancelot Brown in the 1760s. However, this splendid view also contains elements of both earlier and later, organic and planned, landscapes, and the Blenheim Park which we admire today is in reality a palimpsest of many different periods. Figure 7 is an attempt to identify some of the major phases of landscape evolution represented at Blenheim.

The aim of this and the following two chapters is to review the development of the area up to the beginning of the eighteenth century, when the estate came into the hands of the first Duke of Marlborough and the major transformation of the park into its present appearance was commenced by Vanbrugh.

We can distinguish at least three major stages of landscape development underlying the ducal park. First of all we have the relict features of the landscape which existed before any park was created – the earthworks, crop-marks and pottery scatters which represent the remains of prehistoric and Romano-British land boundaries and settlements, features which are most clearly recognisable today towards the northern end of the present park. These early features are the subject of the present chapter. Secondly, we have the medieval royal park, the great hunting-preserve of the Norman and Plantagenet kings, together with the site of the former royal palace and its associated features. The character of the medieval park is to some extent preserved in the wilder south-western quarter of the present park. Thirdly, we have the various fifteenth-, sixteenth- and seventeenth-century additions and extensions which brought the park to the shape which it has now.

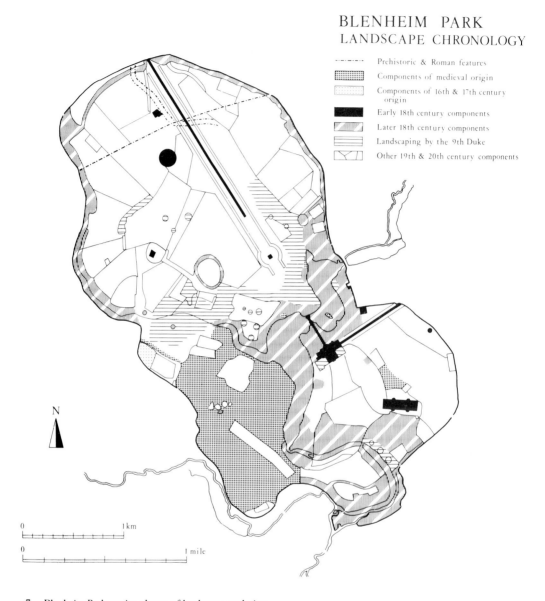

BLENHEIM PARK
LANDSCAPE CHRONOLOGY

- Prehistoric & Roman features
- Components of medieval origin
- Components of 16th & 17th century origin
- Early 18th century components
- Later 18th century components
- Landscaping by the 9th Duke
- Other 19th & 20th century components

N

0   1 km

0   1 mile

7. Blenheim Park: major phases of landscape evolution.

Prehistoric and Roman Landscapes

1. Grim's Ditch

Relict features derived from the earliest periods before the first
creation of a park are most clearly visible on either side of the
present Grand Avenue. One of the earliest and most prominent
archaeological landmarks is a length of bank and ditch, part of
the North Oxfordshire Grim's Ditch, which is a complex system
of linear dykes enclosing an area approaching 5,700 hectares of
countryside between Kiddington, Charlbury and Eynsham. The
short length of earthwork in Blenheim Park represents the
north-easternmost extremity of this extensive system. There has
been much debate over the date and function of this earthwork.
It does appear to enclose a significant group of immensely
wealthy Roman villas, including North Leigh, Fawler, Stonesfield, Shakenoak and Ditchley, and many years ago O.G.S.
Crawford suggested that the Grim's Ditch represented some
sort of late Roman territorial boundary delimiting and protec-
ting this group of important villa estates against Saxon raiders in
the fourth or fifth century.[1] However, the results of a small
excavation carried out in 1936 at the point where the Grim's
Ditch is intersected by Akeman Street were interpreted as
indicating that it was, in fact, of earlier origin, dating from the
first part of the first century A.D. The bank was composed of
cornbrash rubble excavated from the ditch; the ditch was
originally 1.5m deep and 4.9m wide, and the original height from

8.   The excavation of Grim's Ditch in Blenheim Park in 1936:
the bank, with the ditch and Akeman Street beyond.

the ditch bottom to the top of the bank was estimated at about 3.4m; there was no significant berm between them. The bank was laid over the top of an older ploughsoil, and was clearly built across a cultivated landscape; at two excavated points the dyke intersected traces of earlier settlement revealed by pottery dating from the first half of the first century A.D. (including Belgic wares), daub, burnt stones from hearths, food bones and charcoal. The fill of the ditch suggested that it had remained open for a long period, when red silt accumulated in the bottom; subsequently, however, it had been deliberately backfilled, to reduce it as an obstacle. All the sherds in the fill of the ditch were of Roman date.[2]

The Grim's Ditch system bears comparison with the lowland *oppida* constructed by Belgic peoples elsewhere in south-eastern Britain, and it is possibly to be seen as a frontier work on the borders of the territories of the Dobunni to the west and the Catuvellauni to the east.[3] A recent reassessment suggests, however, that the system as a whole is more complex than was originally believed, and may have been constructed in two phases, the section of the earthwork at Blenheim providing vital dating evidence.[4] The state of preservation of the earthwork within Blenheim Park illustrates the advantage which parks have for the archaeologist: inside the park land use has been comparatively stable over a long period, but immediately outside the park wall the earthwork has been almost entirely levelled by cultivation, and only shows up as a cropmark in suitable conditions.

9. The line of Grim's Ditch immediately outside Blenheim Park, revealed by flattened corn after a summer storm, 1974.

10.   Akeman Street cutting across Grim's Ditch in the Great Park: aerial photograph by Major J. Allen, 12 April 1936 (Ashmolean Museum, Oxford).

2.   Akeman Street

The second major archaeological feature at the north end of Blenheim Park is Akeman Street, one of the principal Roman roads of the south midlands, connecting the important Roman towns of Verulamium (St. Alban's) and Corinium (Cirencester).[5] Its alignment through a gap in the Grim's Ditch suggests that here at least it was following the course of an older, unpaved track. Its Roman origin has been recognised at least since the seventeenth century, when Gibson relates that 'Through this Park runs the Consular Way, called Akeman Street, in a raised bank, entering it at Wootton Gate and going out of it at Mapleton Lodge'.[6] Excavation in the park by Haverfield and Grundy in 1898 and by Harden in 1936 has shown that this road was 5.2m wide, with 15–25cm of gravel surfacing on a foundation of larger stones 15–30cm thick. It stood on a broad *agger* 10–16m wide and up to 1m high laid over old ploughsoil, with slight ditches on either side.[7] It is still used as a farm track inside the park, but was blocked off as a public road some time after the Middle Ages, when the park boundary seems to have been extended northwards.

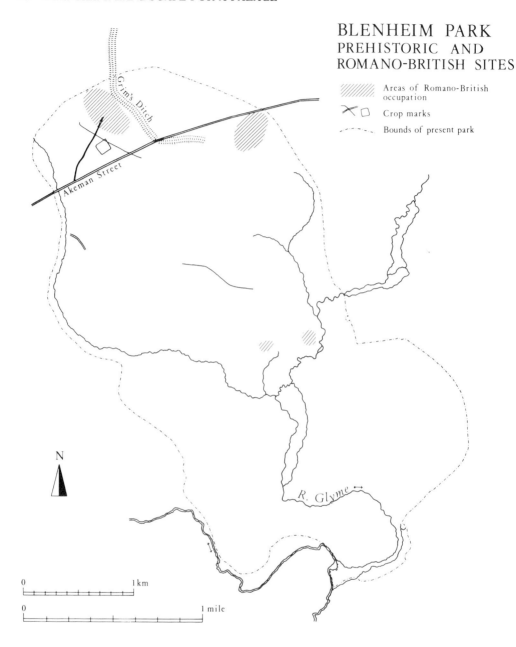

BLENHEIM PARK
PREHISTORIC AND
ROMANO-BRITISH SITES

/////// Areas of Romano-British
        occupation

✕ ▫   Crop marks

- - - - Bounds of present park

11.   Prehistoric and Romano-British sites in Blenheim Park.

12. Akeman Street in the park.

In the seventeenth century Dr. Plot postulated a branch road diverging from Akeman Street in the park near the North Lodge, heading north-westwards past the Callow Hill Roman villa and passing just east of the Wood Farm tumulus, pointing in the general direction of Enstone and Chipping Norton[8]. This theory has generally been dismissed by subsequent generations of archaeologists, since the line of this branch road shown on Plot's map suggests that he had mistaken a length of the bank of the Grim's Ditch for a Roman *agger*.[9] However, the subsequent recognition of a substantial Romano-British settlement at Glyme Farm on the outskirts of Chipping Norton,[10] and clues such as the alignment of a straight length of farm track along the eastern edge of Ditchley Park where it is followed by the parish boundary for half a mile, suggest that Plot's alignment might warrant re-examination.

3.   Romano-British Settlements

A variety of Roman settlements lie alongside or near Akeman Street during its course through west Oxfordshire, and several such settlements can be identified within the present park boundary. Pottery recorded from the ploughsoil on the slopes south-east of Furze Platt suggests the site of a small farmstead, and concentrations of Romano-British pottery have also been found near the Ditchley Lodge and to the north-west of Rosamund's Well. Coins of Vespasian, Gallienus, Tetricus I & II, Carausius, House of Constantine and Valentinian have been found in the park; also a phalera of almost transparent

13. Head of Medusa in chalcedony found in Blenheim Park *c.* 1810 (Ashmolean Museum, Oxford).

chalcedony bearing a low-relief mask of Medusa was found in the park near Akeman Street in 1810.[11] Aerial photography suggests the existence of at least one further farmstead, a rectangular ditched enclosure to the west of the North Lodge, but this site has not yet proved to be particularly prolific in Roman pottery, and its date and function remain uncertain. Roman coins are said to have been found near the site of the medieval royal palace in 1791 and claims have been made for this as the site of a Roman villa;[12] while there is no direct archaeological evidence to support that tradition, there does appear to be a striking gap in the distribution of villas within the Grim's Ditch system in the area of Blenheim Park.[13]

There is ample evidence that the uplands on the west bank of the River Glyme were fully cleared and settled by the Roman period. It remains one of the major puzzles of landscape history in Oxfordshire that an area which was apparently so prosperous and so extensively cultivated at the end of the fourth century should have regressed so far in the space of a few hundred years that it had become a sparsely-inhabited wilderness. No deterministic explanation based on physical geography will suffice; this is in no sense marginal land. There is, however, some evidence to suggest that the Wychwood–Woodstock country may have formed a frontier region for a period during the

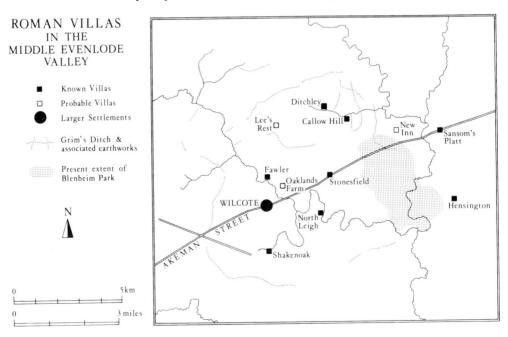

14. Roman villas in the Woodstock area.

emergence of the Anglo-Saxon kingdoms, and a situation can be envisaged whereby cultivated land was falling back to waste in a time of political instability, the resulting secondary woodland then coming to be valued and conserved as a resource in its own right for intercommoning, for supplying wood and timber, and for hunting.[14]

Bibliography

COPELAND T. 1984: 'The North Oxon. Grim's Ditch', *South Midlands Archaeology* Vol. 14, pp. 100–103.

COPELAND T. 1988: 'The North Oxfordshire Grim's Ditch: a fieldwork survey', *Oxoniensia* Vol. 53, pp. 277–292.

CRAWFORD O.G.S. 1930: 'Grim's Ditch in Wychwood, Oxon.', *Antiquity* Vol. 4 (No. 15), pp. 303–315.

HARDEN D.B. 1937: 'Excavations on Grim's Ditch, North Oxfordshire', *Oxoniensia* Vol. 2, pp. 74–92 (esp. pp. 80–90).

HAVERFIELD F. 1899: 'Notes on excavation of Roman road in Blenheim Park', *Proc. Soc. of Antiq. of London* (2nd ser.) Vol. 17, pp. 333–335.

MARSHALL E. 1873: *The Early History of Woodstock Manor and its Environs* (James Parker & Co., Oxford).

PLOT R. 1705: *The Natural History of Oxfordshire* (2nd edn., Oxford).

SCHUMER B. 1984: *The Evolution of Wychwood to 1400: Pioneers, Frontiers and Forests* (Leicester University Dept. of English Local History, Occasional Papers, 3rd ser. No. 6).

References & Footnotes

1   CRAWFORD O.G.S. 1930: Crawford's estimates of the contemporary extent of woodland cannot be accepted in the light of subsequent research.

2   HARDEN D.B. 1937.

3   HARDING D.W. 1972: *The Iron Age in the Upper Thames Basin* (Oxford University Press), pp. 56–60.

4   COPELAND T. 1984; also COPELAND T. 1988 in which (pp. 281–2) he argues two phases of construction, both Iron Age, the first bordering an area of around 13 square km., the second a territory of some 80 square km. 'The evidence suggests that the Ditch was probably constructed in the late Iron Age, and that Phase Two fell into disuse in the early Roman period. The critical evidence comes from the excavations at Blenheim.' See also Harden 1937.

5   MARGARY I.D. 1967: *Roman Roads in Britain* (John Baker, London, revised edn.), pp. 155–162.

6   GIBSON E. (ed., 1695), CAMDEN W.: *Britannia*, p. 271.

7   HAVERFIELD F. 1899; HARDEN D.B. 1937.

8   PLOT R. 1705, pp. 328 & 333.

9   The Victoria History of the Counties of England (henceforward V.C.H.), Oxfordshire, Vol. I (1939), p. 276.

10   EDDERSHAW D.G.T. 1972: 'Roman finds at Glyme Farm, Chipping Norton', *Oxoniensia* Vol. 37, p. 242.

11   V.C.H. Oxon I (1939) pp. 332–333.

12   MAVOR W. 1806: *New Description of Blenheim* (6th edn., p. 116n; GODWIN 1867: *English Archaeologists' Handbook* (Oxford), p. 321; MARSHALL 1873, p. 13.

13   I am grateful to Tim Copeland for this observation.

14   *Cf.* STURDY D. 1963: 'Traces of Saxon Nomadic Life near Oxford', *Oxoniensia* Vol. 28, pp. 95–98; SCHUMER 1984.

4. WOODSTOCK PARK IN THE MIDDLE AGES

James Bond

Park and Forest in the Middle Ages

THE DOMESDAY Survey gives the impression that, by the late eleventh century, a considerable tract of land in central west Oxfordshire had become uncultivated and sparsely populated. There is no indication of any town or village at Woodstock. Instead, we are told that 'In Shotover, Stowood, Woodstock, Cornbury and Wychwood, the King's demesne forests have nine leagues in length and the same in breadth. . . From them and everything belonging to the forest, Rainald renders yearly to the king £10.'[1] The circumstances by which land at Woodstock came into possession of the Crown are not wholly clear. There is a somewhat insubstantial tradition that King Alfred had a residence here, where he is said to have translated Boethius's *De Consolatione Philosophiae* in the 880s, but this seems unlikely, since Woodstock lay within the bounds of Mercia rather than Wessex. There is a more positive record of King Ethelred holding a meeting of the Witan here.[2] However, whether these rather shadowy references can be taken to imply direct links between the important late Roman villa estates in the area and the medieval royal preserve must remain for the moment a matter of speculation.

15. Woodstock and the Oxfordshire forests in Domesday Book, 1086.

'Forest' in the Middle Ages was primarily a legal concept, an area reserved for the royal hunt, where Forest Law took precedence over Common Law. It did not necessarily imply an area entirely blanketed with dense woodland. Forests often included open country, cultivated land, farms and villages.[3] Nonetheless, most medieval royal forests did include a substantial nucleus of woodland or wood-pasture. The existence of a considerable tract of such countryside within easy reach of London and Oxford proved a great attraction to the Norman and Plantagenet kings, and this royal interest in the area was to exercise a profound effect upon its development over the next few centuries.

The records of later medieval chroniclers suggest that it was King Henry I who made the first enclosure of the park at Woodstock towards the beginning of the twelfth century,[4] though no direct contemporary evidence for this tradition has yet been found. Woodstock appears to be the earliest of over thirty parks created in Oxfordshire during the Middle Ages, and it remained the largest and most important.[5] While such parks are fairly widely distributed throughout the county, there is something of a concentration of them in western Oxfordshire, in the environs of Wychwood Forest (fig. 17). It is more difficult to be positive about the chronology of their creation. Their first appearance in the documentary record may postdate their first appearance in the landscape by many decades. Even sources such as imparking licences are not wholly reliable – sometimes such licences were acquired merely to legalise a long-established situation, while on other occasions they appear to represent a declaration of intent, which might be long delayed in its fulfilment. However, from the evidence available, it would appear that the main period of park creation in Oxfordshire occurs in the later twelfth and thirteenth centuries (fig. 16).

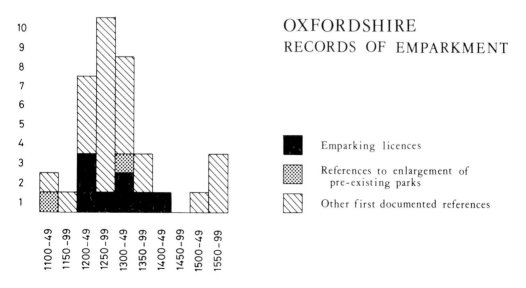

OXFORDSHIRE
RECORDS OF EMPARKMENT

■ Emparking licences

▦ References to enlargement of pre-existing parks

◪ Other first documented references

16.   The chronology of Oxfordshire parks in the Middle Ages.

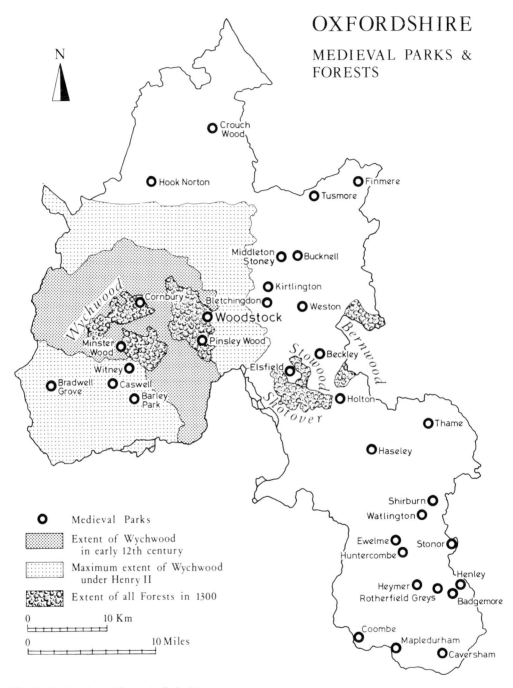

17.   Medieval parks and forests in Oxfordshire.

Deer in the Park

The main purpose of the medieval park was quite different from the modern concept of the term. It was in no sense intended to be an ornamental landscape, a fine setting for a great house or palace. Instead, it had a much more mundane function, that of providing and maintaining a regular supply of venison for the table. Deer provided an important source of animal protein when other livestock had to be killed off before winter, and the hunting of the deer was a popular form of recreation for the royal household.

It is difficult to estimate the number of deer which Woodstock Park may have contained at any one time. Between 1230 and 1300 there are records of well over a thousand deer being taken in the park, but there are also a number of rather vaguely-defined grants allowing various people to take unspecified numbers of deer from the park every year, and the total number of kills was probably very much greater.[6] The first indication of stocking occurs in 1577, when Henry Lee, Ranger of Woodstock, was expected to maintain a herd of 2,000–3,000 deer in the park.[7] Even allowing for the fact that hay from the royal meadows was being diverted towards their keep, this seems a very large number for the size of the enclosure.

Some of the medieval kings came frequently to Woodstock to hunt, and on occasions they permitted other people to enjoy the resources there: in 1303 Edward de Balliol was allowed to take one deer in the park 'for sport'.[8] Primarily, however, the park served as a royal larder. Throughout much of the thirteenth century the Close Rolls and Liberate Rolls record a succession of orders sent out by the king between September and May to his huntsmen to take deer, to salt down the venison, and to despatch it to the king wherever he happened to be.[9] In 1250, for example, 200 does were killed in Woodstock Park, 12s. 8d. was spent on salting them down, and half was sent to Winchester for Christmas, the other half to Westminster for the Feast of St. Edward.[10] In 1298 the Keeper of Woodstock Manor was ordered to capture 100 does in the park, and when he had killed twenty or thirty, to salt them down, pack them in barrels and deliver them to the king at York[11] – clearly transporting the venison over considerable distances was no object, though there would have been alternative sources of supply much closer to hand. Gifts of deer for food to various institutions and individuals are also frequently recorded: in 1444, for example, Henry VI granted to Abingdon Abbey the right to have annually four bucks and two does from Woodstock Park, partially in lieu

18.   King John hunting: based on a fourteenth-century illustration.

of the abbey's former right to deer from Windsor Forest. Windsor was too far away from Abingdon, and it was said that the deer previously delivered had often been 'unseasonable, to the great cost of the abbey'.[12] There are regular records of the Abbess of Godstow receiving a tithe of 'soul-silver' on venison taken in the park.[13]

Woodstock Park, because of its comparatively large size, was also one of the most important local sources of live deer for restocking other parks in central Oxfordshire. In 1203 the king gave Gerard de Camville ten bucks and forty does from Woodstock to stock his park at Middleton Stoney. In 1280 Henry de Lacy received a similar grant of fifteen does for the same park; and in 1295 de Lacy was to have six bucks and ten does from Woodstock Park and other deer from Wychwood and Beckley.[14] If Middleton Stoney appears to resemble a bottom-less pit as far as deer were concerned, this may underline the difficulties of maintaining a viable herd in a too-limited area. On other occasions, live deer were moved over distances of twenty miles or more from Woodstock; it would be of interest to know exactly how they were transported.[15]

Poaching was a regular problem.[15] In 1295 Ralph de Slape was imprisoned for 'trespass of venison' in Woodstock Park,[16] and in 1413 it is recorded that the scholars of the University of Oxford had made such a nuisance of themselves through stealing deer, hares and rabbits there that they were prohibited from entering the park entirely.[17]

The Park Boundary

Deer are capable of leaping a considerable obstacle – up to 6m horizontally, or up to 3m vertically. If deer were to be contained within the park and kept from straying onto neighbouring cultivated ground, there was a need for the enclosure to have a formidable boundary. The usual form of medieval park boundary consisted of a massive bank topped by a wooden paling fence, with a ditch on the *interior* side to deny the animals a suitable take-off point from which to leap the barrier.

If the earliest park enclosure was significantly smaller in extent than the present area of Blenheim, then it ought to be possible to find some trace of its bounds in view of the substantial earthworks required. However, the field evidence has been much disturbed by later modifications to the landscape, and its interpretation has been further complicated both by a confusing sequence of additions to the original enceinte and by the existence of internal boundaries of varying dates within the park.

Traces of the earliest park boundary have proved remarkably elusive. What at first appeared to be a classic length of prominent bank and internal ditch on the western edge of Blenheim, separating the High Park from the area known as 'New Park', is now known to have lain entirely outside the bounds of the medieval enclosure. It appears instead to represent the boundary of a rabbit warren created upon former arable land cut out of the open fields of Combe and added to the park in about 1780.

Further south, on the break of slope overlooking the Glyme valley, vestiges of a hedgerow on top of a bank with a ditch on its northern side can still be traced along the line of the Bladon

19. This prominent bank and ditch between the High Park and New Park resembles the classic form of medieval park pale, but it is now known to have lain entirely outside the medieval park, and may be a later rabbit-warren boundary.

parish boundary, though now almost ploughed out; but again, although this resembles the appearance of a medieval park boundary, it now seems more likely to relate to the extensions carried out by Sir Henry Lee in the sixteenth century.

The northern limits of the medieval park, originally thought to lie south of the Akeman Street, are now believed to coincide with the present park wall. On the eastern side a case could be made on topographical grounds for the original boundary following the top of the steep slope between the Icehouse Clump and Fishery Cottage, where a slight terrace is clearly discernible – this slope, with a wall or fence along its top, would have provided a very effective barrier, which would have kept deer out of the crofts of Old Woodstock, some of which may have been taken into the park at a later date. However, there are also difficulties with this interpretation, as will be discussed below. On balance it is now difficult to point to any part of the course of the medieval park boundary which has escaped destruction.

One of the unusual features of Woodstock Park was its stone boundary wall instead of the more usual paling fence. It is not known whether this was an original feature. Although the fifteenth-century chronicler John Rous speaks of Henry I enclosing the park with a stone wall, he was probably describing the circumstances of his own time. However, despite the absence of any contemporary record of its first construction, the wall was certainly in being by the early thirteenth century. According to Rous's account the medieval park wall was 7 miles (c. 11.3km) in circumference.[18] Total reliance cannot be placed upon the length quoted. Nonetheless this would represent an area quite appreciably smaller than that of Blenheim Park where the present wall approaches 14.5km in circumference.

The maintenance of the stone wall was a constant problem. In 1232 the custodian of Woodstock Park was ordered to permit the men of the neighbouring villages to close and repair the breaches in the park wall with stone, in order that their animals should not enter and other animals should not escape from the park.[19] In 1250 it was ordered that the wall of the king's park towards the town should be raised, and that it should be repaired in another place.[20] Five years later a jury representing the inhabitants of the surrounding demesne townships complained 'with one voice, that the park wall is not built as it ought to be': it was claimed that twenty-two oaks had been felled in Stonesfield Wood and another thirty-two in Bloxham Wood to fuel kilns making lime for the park wall, but that the lime from

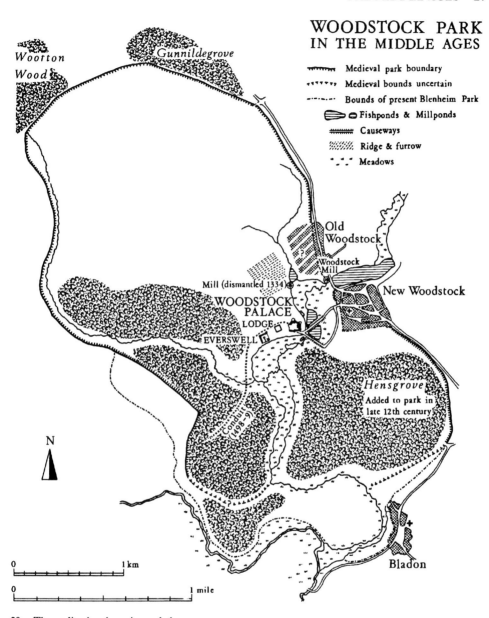

WOODSTOCK PARK
IN THE MIDDLE AGES

〜〜〜 Medieval park boundary

‹‹‹‹‹‹ Medieval bounds uncertain

—·—·— Bounds of present Blenheim Park

⬭ ⬮ Fishponds & Millponds

▥ Causeways

▨ Ridge & furrow

Meadows

Wootton Wood

Gunnildegrove

Old Woodstock

Woodstock Mill

Mill (dismantled 1334)

New Woodstock

WOODSTOCK PALACE

LODGE

EVERSWELL

Hensgrove
Added to park in
late 12th century

Conduit (1498-9)

N

Bladon

0   1 km

0   1 mile

20. The medieval park; conjectural plan.

the kilns was not used for the wall as it should have been . . . 'They say that part of the lime was used to plaster the wall, but that it immediately fell off . . . and that all the lime used for the wall did not profit the king one halfpenny . . . They say that they gave for each perch of the wall to be built 3s. 6d. at first, and afterwards 3s., and that the work was badly done, and that each perch might have been better built for 2s. 6d..'[21] Repairs to the park wall and palings – which might suggest that not all the circuit was walled in stone – are regularly recorded throughout the later thirteenth and early fourteenth centuries.[22] Maintaining a stone park wall must always have presented difficulties, but the prestige of Woodstock was such that owners of certain other parks nearby were soon imitating it: Beckley Park was walled with stone in 1192–7, Middleton Stoney Park in 1328, and Cornbury Park similarly before 1337.[23]

When a park adjoined other wooded country where wild deer might live, the boundary might be equipped with one or more *deer-leaps.* These were essentially one-way gates, which allowed deer to enter the park from the surrounding woods, but prevented their exit. They took a variety of forms, but one of the simplest types is illustrated from Wolseley Park in Staffordshire, where a gap in the palings was spanned by rails, with a broad pit on the interior side.[24] Owners of private parks normally needed to obtain royal permission before erecting a deer-leap, but since Woodstock Park was in royal ownership anyway, it could be equipped without special licence. In 1251 there is a record of oak timber being cut in the *boscus forinsecus*, the woodland outside the park boundary, in order to make a deer-leap.[25] In 1256 it was ordered that the deer-leaps between Woodstock

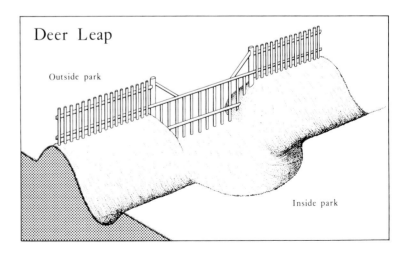

21. One type of deer-leap.

Park and the forest should be opened to allow beasts of the chase to enter and exit freely until the next Feast of the Assumption[26] – is this an attempt to improve the quality of the stock by allowing in fresh blood to prevent undue inbreeding, or does it represent an attempt to vary the style of entertainment by opening up the option of hunting the deer across the countryside outside the park? In 1301 there was an order for two deer-leaps to be made in Woodstock Park.[27] As yet, the sites of none of the recorded deer-leaps have been located on the ground.

Other Park Livestock

Although deer represented the *raison d'être* of the park, it also contained other livestock. In connection with the royal hunt, in 1250 the bailiff of Woodstock had the custody of an eyrie of falcons in the park, and at least one local tenant held his lands by the service of carrying feed to the king's falcons there.[28] Part of the royal stud was also housed for a time at Woodstock: it is mentioned on at least ten separate occasions between 1254 and 1361.[29] The stables are referred to in 1254 and 1325;[30] and in 1334 there is a record of straw, hay and litter being brought for the king's stud.[31] In 1361, however, it was ordered that all the horses and mares in the royal stud at Woodstock should be sold, and there appears to be no subsequent record after this dispersal.[32]

Rights of common grazing which existed before the first enclosure of the park seem to have survived to some degree well into the thirteenth century. Pannage, the payment from tenants for the privilege of turning out swine to forage on the manorial waste, was still significant at Woodstock at this period, although in many other places it had lost much of the importance attached to it at the time of the Domesday survey. In 1254 four persons are reported to have had 164 pigs in the park, and in 1279 more than 600 pigs were turned out into the park for the mast season,

22. Acorns for the pigs: based on a late thirteenth-century illustration.

yielding £2 10s.[33] In 1252 acorns totalling 40s. in value were collected in the park, and two years later the bailiff had girls collecting acorns worth 4s. a week.[34] Also after the mid–thirteenth century there are references to cattle and plough-oxen being pastured within the park: in 1254, for example, there were seventy oxen and twelve cows.[35] In 1501 the keeper of the king's garden at Woodstock was allowed grass for one cow and one horse within the park,[36] and in the third quarter of the sixteenth century Sir Henry Lee was still entitled to keep seventy head of cattle and forty horses on the demesnes, probably a continuation of the ancient pasture rights of commoners and park officers.[37]

Wild livestock other than deer are recorded only incidentally. In 1261, for example, there was an order for the extermination of the foxes and badgers which were causing damage to the park.[38] The most exotic element of the medieval park was the menagerie established there by Henry I. William of Malmesbury's chronicle records that Henry 'was extremely fond of the wonders of different countries, begging with great delight from foreign kings lions, leopards, lynxes and camels, animals which England does not produce. He had a park called Woodstock, in which he used to foster his favourites of this kind. He had placed there also a creature called a porcupine, sent to him by William of Montpellier. . .'.[39]

Mills and Fishponds

Any medieval park needed a spring or stream or river running through it, to provide water for the deer and other stock. Woodstock Park included several fresh springs and streamlets, and in its earliest form its eastern boundary seems to have abutted upon the River Glyme; subsequently it was extended to include land on the east bank of the Glyme also. Given that a supply of water was present within the enclosed area, the opportunity could then be taken to utilise it for a variety of other purposes.

Fishponds were a ubiquitous feature of the medieval landscape, and frequently occur as an adjunct to parks. The first known record at Woodstock occurs in 1227, when Brother Ralph, lay-brother of St. James of Northampton, was sent to Woodstock to repair the king's fishpond there.[40] A constant string of documentary references then occurs through to about 1340.

The earliest sources refer only to a single pond, but the system was almost certainly extended more than once. By 1242 the bailiff of Woodstock was being ordered to repair the causeway between the king's two fish-stews,[41] and in 1252 John de Hanborough and Peter de Leigh, keepers of the king's works at Woodstock, were ordered to make a third stewpond in the king's garden.[42] In 1256 the stewpond in the garden was to be surrounded by a hedge.[43] The layout of the ponds is not known for certain, but they presumably occupied a considerable part of the valley-bottom. It is of some interest that the plan of the park in 1725 in *Vitruvius Britannicus* shows two very large ponds in the Glyme valley, predating Lancelot Brown's lake by nearly forty years.[44] There is no other evidence to confirm the presence of an extensive water-body in the park at this time, and it is probable that the plan shows only a suggested landscaping scheme; nonetheless, it is just possible that the outline of the two lakes might have been suggested by the still-discernible vestiges of the royal fishponds. While these would have been unusually large compared with most medieval pond systems, they were probably not impossibly so; and that at least one of the medieval ponds was of some size is suggested by the order to the bailiff in 1259 to fell one good oak in the park to make a boat for the king's fishpond.[45] The documentation referring to the fishponds falls into six main categories:

i.   *Maintenance and repair of ponds.* There are regular records of repairs.[46] In 1249 the bailiff was ordered 'to repair the bays of both the fish stews and the dam of the lower stew by the sluice,' and three years later oak timber was allowed from the park to repair the sluices of the stews 'which are again broken down'.[47] In 1334 a major overhaul of the works along the valley included the raising of the head of one of the fishponds and the repair of the causeways.[48]

ii.   *Stocking.* The only types of fish recorded at Woodstock are pike and eels, in contrast to other royal ponds such as Feckenham (Worcestershire), which seem to have specialised in

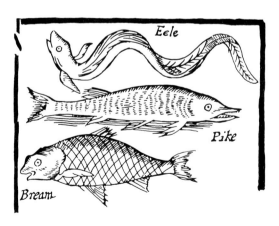

23.   Eel, pike and bream, as illustrated in H. Woolley, *The Accomplisht Ladys Delight.* 6th ed.[n], 1686.

the production of bream. In 1241 the bailiff was requested 'to buy 1000 pike wherever he can find them, to stock the king's stew of Woodstock'; in 1301 500 pike were bought to stock the Woodstock ponds; and in 1304 the bailiff was to acquire a further 100 great pike to put into the stews.[49] In 1256 sixty bream were taken from the king's fishpond at Marlborough and sent to Woodstock,[50] but these were probably destined directly for the king's table, rather than for stocking the ponds.

iii.   *Exploitation.* In 1253 William, the king's fisherman, was ordered to take six pike in the king's fishpond at Woodstock.[51] In 1271–2 the fisherman was to take fish from the upper stew at Woodstock and send them to the king in parcels.[52]

iv.   *Maintenance of fishing equipment.* In 1272 the bailiffs of Oxford were ordered to give 10s. to two of the king's fishermen at Woodstock for the repair of their nets, lately broken in the king's service.[53]

v.   *Gifts.* In 1251 the bailiff was requested to allow Guy de Rochford one pike from the fishpond at Woodstock, by gift of the king. Eels in the ponds were granted to Osney Abbey in 1231.[54]

vi.   *Poaching.* In 1298 Geoffrey le Stedeman was in the king's prison at Oxford Castle for trespass in the fishpond at Woodstock.[55]

Where water could be dammed up to create fishponds, it could also be made to drive mills. Just below the modern Fishery Cottage, at the point where the arm of the lake containing the numerous small islets narrows before opening out into the present Queen Pool, two bands of stonework project a couple of metres out into the lake from the bank, and on the adjoining land below the park road slight earthworks are visible. These features were not fully understood until the long, dry summer of

24.   The medieval mill-dam, 1976.

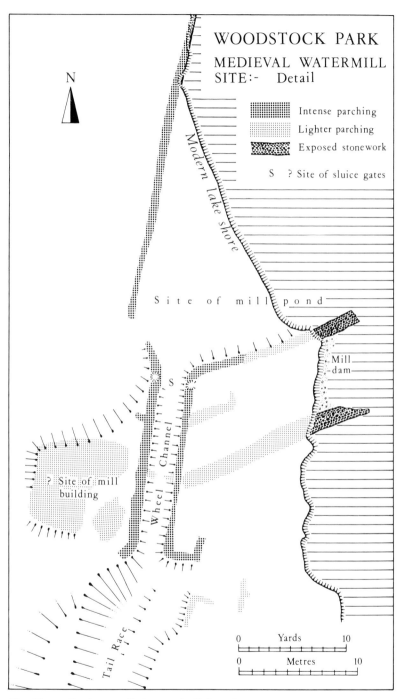

25.   The medieval watermill site near the Fishery Cottage.

26.   Parchmarks showing the wheel channel and tail race of the medieval watermill, summer 1976.

27.   Stone revetment of the medieval mill pond exposed on the lake shore below the Fishery Cottage.

1976, when a fall in the lake level made it possible to identify the two parallel bands of stonework as the revetment of a clay dam, and the appearance of parch-marks on the grass made it possible to trace the outline of a stone-lined pond, a stone-lined wheel channel and a building platform, while a band of still-verdant grass along a slight hollow identified the course of the tail-race of what can only have been a vanished water-mill.[56] On 11 July 1334 Edward III ordered John de Hanborough, keeper of the works of the manor of Woodstock, to remove 'a certain water-mill now erected in Woodstock Park' and 'to cause it to be re-erected in a suitable place without the park',[57] very probably on the site of the present Woodstock Mill, which lies immediately outside the modern park wall. No other mill within the medieval park bounds is known, either from field evidence or from the documentary record, and there is a very strong case for identifying the site below the Fishery Cottage with the site of the mill demolished in 1334. Although the valley above the Fishery Cottage is now dry, it is likely that in the Middle Ages, when the water-table was higher, it would have contained sufficient of a stream to provide the necessary head of water; alternatively a contour leat could have been fed into the millpond from the Glyme itself, and some of the early eighteenth-century plans of the park indicate that such a leat once existed.

Meadowland and Reed-beds

Away from the fishponds the valley-bottom was partly occupied by reed-beds, a valuable resource for thatching: in 1254 the reed-beds were said to be worth 7s.[58] There were also several meadows within the park boundary, where the king's tenants owed mowing and carrying services. In the late thirteenth century the tenants of Bladon had to mow a meadow called Law Mead in the park for one day, and in 1369 the manor of Stanton Harcourt was said to be held by services which included mowing the king's meadow in Woodstock Park and lifting and carrying the hay;[59] as late as 1551 the customary tenants of Hanborough, Combe and Bladon still owed mowing and haymaking services and the lord of Stanton Harcourt was still obliged to find someone to mow and carry hay from Stanton and Southlye Mead in the park.[60]

Wood-pasture

The most characteristic form of landscape within the medieval park was the type of open wood-pasture which is still preserved to a considerable degree in the south-western quarter around High Lodge and the Combe Gate. Numerous ancient pollarded oaks survive here, interspersed with glades of rough grassland, and there can be little doubt that this is, in essence, the direct descendant of the medieval forest. No less than twelve vascular plants and sixteen lichens which are regarded as locally-reliable indicator-species of ancient woodland have been recorded here. This is the highest total for any tetrad in Oxfordshire, Berkshire or Buckinghamshire. Archaeological evidence supports the view that this was the very heart of the medieval park: several fourteenth- and fifteenth-century arrowheads have been found in this area in the past. Even now the High Park has a slightly sinister air about it, with the gaunt and skeletal crowns of the stag-headed oaks clawing their way skywards, and it may well have been deliberately retained in this form as a foil to the tamer, more orderly landscape closer to the duke's palace. Certainly, viewed from the Triumphal Arch, it provides an effective backdrop to Brown's lake and Vanbrugh's bridge, its dark tones and rougher texture contrasting vividly with the smoother, brighter carpets of grassland in the foreground.

28.   Colonel's Oak, near Combe Lodge: photograph by Henry Taunt, *c.* 1900.

Timber and wood was an important secondary product of the medieval park. It was especially important as a reserve of

29. An outsized oak in the High Park: photograph by Henry Taunt, *c.* 1900.

ancient, outsized trees, which might be invaluable for some construction operations, but which were not normally found in woodlands managed primarily for timber and coppice products.[61]

i. *Building timber.* Between 1232 and 1284 there are over twenty references to the use of oaks from Woodstock Park for building, recording the felling of at least ninety trees. A considerable proportion of the recorded grants are gifts to religious houses in Oxford. In 1275 Godstow Nunnery received fifteen oaks and the Carmelite Friars and Austin Friars of Oxford ten oaks each; two years later the Oxford Blackfriars received six oaks.[62] The park also provided timber for some of the king's own works: in 1232 three oaks were taken to make a porch at Woodstock Palace itself, in 1272 two oaks were carried away to provide tie-beams in the hall of Beaumont Palace, and in 1283 four oaks were requisitioned for works at Oxford Castle.[63]

ii. *Other wood for building works.* In addition to structural timbers, in 1256 the park provided four oaks for laths for Woodstock Palace. The accounts for the roofing of the chambers and hall in the steward's court of the palace in 1265 included 2*d.* paid 'for 2,000 wooden nails'. In 1275 timber from Woodstock was sent to Brill in Buckinghamshire, to provide shingles for the king's manor-house there.[64]

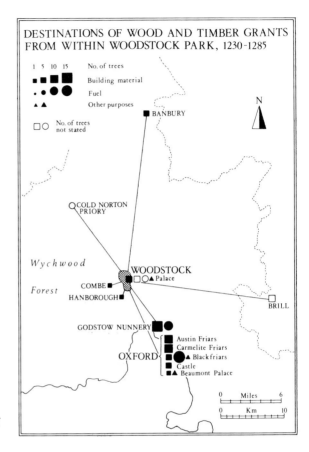

DESTINATIONS OF WOOD AND TIMBER GRANTS
FROM WITHIN WOODSTOCK PARK, 1230-1285

30.   Grants by Henry III and Edward I of
wood and timber from Woodstock Park.

iii   *Furniture.* There are several references to the use of wood
from the park for making furniture. In 1264, for example, the
Sheriff of Oxford had three oaks to make tables, benches and
stools for Beaumont Palace.[65]

iv.   *Fuel.* The tenants of some of the neighbouring manors
retained rights of estover in the park: in 1279, for example, the
tenants of Bladon could take away a faggot of wood as big as
they could lift with an axe in exchange for each day's service of
cutting ivy and mowing in the park.[66] The palace itself
consumed a great deal of firewood when the king was in
residence. In 1232 firewood was in such short supply that it was
ordered that no more should be taken from the park itself, and
the forester was requested to have brushwood cut and charcoal
made in Wychwood outside the park and sent to Woodstock
before each royal visit. In 1256 no less than 500 cartloads of
firewood and 150 quarters of charcoal were sent to Woodstock
Palace.[67] Despite this, gifts of fuel are also recorded, and

religious houses are again prominent amongst the recipients: the Oxford Blackfriars received four trees for fuel in 1275, six more in 1276, and another six in 1277, while the Prior of Cold Norton received thirty cartloads of brushwood from the park in 1277.[68]

v.   *Browse-wood.* In the late thirteenth and fourteenth centuries tenants in Bladon, Combe, Stanton Harcourt and other surrounding manors owed the king the service of cutting ivy, foliage and twigs of shredded or pollarded trees within the park to supply extra feed for the deer in winter whenever the snow lay on the ground for more than two or three days.[69] Some of these services remained current, at least in theory, into the sixteenth century.[70]

There is little direct evidence for the management of the park woodland. As far as one can gather, the park consisted mostly of uncompartmented wood-pasture, without any significant extent of coppice. There are occasional thirteenth-century references

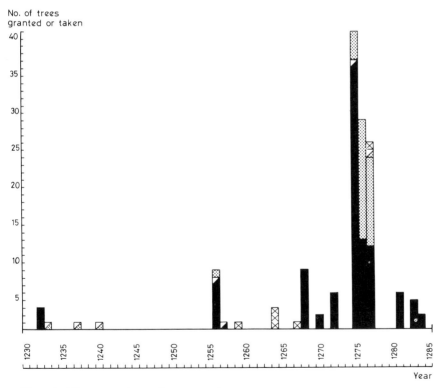

31. The use of timber and wood from Woodstock Park, 1230–1285.

to what sounds like pollarding. In general the records of timber and firewood grants suggest a very haphazard and spasmodic pattern of felling. Only for one period, 1274–1277, is there any evidence for large-scale clearance. Edward I spent Christmas of 1274 at Woodstock, and planned the extensive felling of *trenchea* (presumably rides) in the park and in the wood of Hensigrove on the east bank of the Glyme.[71]

The Royal Palace

The focal point of the medieval park was the hunting-lodge or manor-house, built (or, perhaps, rebuilt) by Henry I. The earliest buildings were probably of timber, and in 1129–30 47*s*. were spent on 'shingles and laths for covering the king's buildings at Woodstock'. It was Henry II who began the expansion of this park lodge into a full-scale royal palace, and the range of buildings which grew up around the original nucleus is well-documented. The twelfth-century hall was much altered by Henry III. At first-floor level at one end of the hall the king's high chamber was decorated with wall-paintings and had a green-painted wainscot, door and window-shutters. The queen's apartments included a vaulted whitewashed chamber, and in 1252 one of the queen's rooms was painted green with a red border. By the time of Henry III the palace contained no less than six oratories or chapels, including a round one which may have been similar to that still surviving at Ludlow Castle. There were also extensive outbuildings, including a kitchen, buttery, larder, wine-cellar, almonry, stables, smithy, dovecote and gatehouse. The early timber buildings appear to have been progressively replaced in stone, and in 1241 Henry III ordered all the buildings there to be roofed with local stone slates.

The pace of augmentation and embellishment of the buildings seems to have slowed down after the later thirteenth

32.   The earliest known depiction of the Royal Palace at Woodstock, by Daniel King, 1665. By permission of the British Library, BL. K. Top. XXXV 28.a.

33. The twelfth-century chapel at Ludlow Castle, Shropshire. The round chapel at Woodstock Palace may have been similar.

century, although occasional additions continue to be recorded. In 1354 a new chamber was built and a timber balcony constructed outside the chamber of Princess Isabella to give her a view over the park. Early in the following century a new tower was begun by the entrance to the king's chamber, which took thirty years to complete: the finishing touches were applied in 1439–41, when ten great slabs of Taynton stone were bought and a man named Stephen was paid £3 6s. 8d. for carving lions and antelopes on them to ornament the new tower.[72]

The subsequent decay and destruction of the medieval royal palace will be discussed briefly in the following chapter. Today there are only two reminders of its site. The more obvious is the small stone tablet erected by the Oxfordshire Architectural and Historical Society on the bluff facing the new palace of Blenheim on the opposite side of the valley. A more subtle clue is provided by the alignment of Queen Elizabeth's Island in the lake. Visitors coming to the royal palace from the direction of London or Oxford had to approach it across one of two causeways which spanned the marshy floor of the Glyme valley. The northernmost causeway continued the line of Park Street in the town of New Woodstock, approaching the palace from the north-east. The second causeway may have served as one of the dams of the fishponds described earlier. It was first recorded in 1240, and repaired in 1242; in 1334 Edward II reserved money for the repair of both the causeways at Woodstock.[73] The ruins of the southern causeway were still sufficiently prominent in the 1760s to persuade Lancelot Brown to accommodate them as an ornamental feature in his lake, and the central section now forms the long island. In the dry summer of 1976, when the lake level fell, the ruined abutment of the causeway was seen as an outcrop of loose stone on the shore below the old palace.

34. 'The King's Manner House at Woodstock' from the King George III Geographical and Topographical Collection. By permission of the British Library, BL. K. Top. XXXV 28.e.

35.   An engraving of 1714, based upon the above drawing (reversed).

36. Tablet erected on the site of the Royal Palace.

37. The ruined abutment of the causeway below the medieval palace site, summer 1976.

Other Medieval Park Buildings

Bowers or pleasaunces, which served to provide an escape from the formality of court life, frequently occur as an adjunct to medieval palaces. In 1165 we have the first reference to a spring called Everswell in Woodstock Park, which fed some of the king's fishponds.[74] Henry II saw the potential of this site, and began its development as a bower. Here, according to popular tradition, he installed his mistress, Rosamund de Clifford, and the spring is known today as 'Fair Rosamund's Well'.[75] By the fifteenth century there was a suite of rooms and a cloister surrounding a paved courtyard, through which the spring waters were led through a flight of three pools. A chapel with painted walls adjoined the buildings. A herb garden was made there in about 1230, and in 1264 a hundred pear trees were planted around the bower, probably because of the attractiveness of their blossom rather than for their fruit.[76] Howard Colvin has suggested that there may be an attempt to recreate in these enclosed pools and orchards the scene described in the well-known twelfth-century romance of Tristan and Iseult, one version of which was probably written for Henry II himself; it is also reminiscent of the rural pavilions and water-gardens built by the Norman kings in Sicily, inspired by Arab garden designs.[77] This pleasant spot fell into disuse after the fifteenth century, and in 1577 the house and dovecote at Rosamund's

38. Fair Rosamund's Well today.

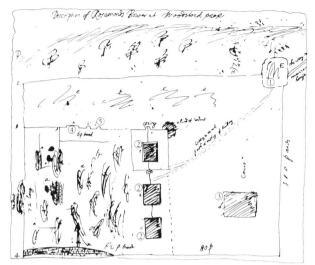

Ruins at Rosamund's Well
John Aubrey's sketch plan

① "Ruines of a noble gatehouse or Tower of Entrance"

② "Three Baths in trayne"

③ "a pond in the Court"

④ "seems to have been a seat in the wall about 2 yards long"

⑤ "Two niches, one very much ruined"

39. John Aubrey's drawing of Rosamund's Well.

Well were said to be in ruins. However, some elements can be deciphered on a sketch plan of the ruins made by John Aubrey in the seventeenth century. Today only one pool remains below the spring, within an open square paved area – the Gothick bathing-house proposed for the site in the 1770s was never erected. However, the uneven ground along the lakeside around the spring conceals the foundations of the medieval buldings, many odd scraps of pottery (mostly of fourteenth- to sixteenth-century date) have been turned up here by the activities of moles, and at one point on the shore a small area of pitched stone paving can be seen disappearing beneath the waters of the lake.[78] In recent years the spring at Rosamund's Well provided the initial source for Blenheim mineral water, bottled and marketed by the estate. Supplies are now drawn from a newly sunk and more prolific bore hole at Park Farm.

Henry VII's building at Woodstock in 1498–9 included extensive waterworks, with a conduit to carry supplies, presumably for the great fountain in the main courtyard of the

40, 41. Squared masonry and pitched stone paving from the medieval buildings at Rosamund's Well, exposed in the lake shore.

palace and for baths there. Water was drawn from springs on high ground on the west of the park, towards Combe, and carried partly in tunnels and partly in pipes enclosed in wood on stone piers across Combe Bottom to a cistern house.[79]

When the king was not in residence, the park was normally maintained by a keeper or bailiff. In 1337 there was 'a House called "Logge"' built of stone and timber which provided accommodation for the parkers.[80] This was possibly on the site of High Lodge, which is first recorded under this name in 1577 when it was in the tenure of Henry Lee, who then held the post of Ranger of Woodstock. The original High Lodge stood immediately west of the Palace, not on the site of the present lodge of that name.

In 1463 three lodges are recorded in the three launds of the park. It seems likely that these were the 'central' lodge known as High Lodge, Gorrel and New Lodges. In 1577 four lodges are named: High Lodge, 'Bladen Lodge' in 'Hernegrove' (Hensgrove), Gorrel and New Lodges. A fifth lodge was built in the Straights in 1586–71.[81] These presumably provided accommodation for park officers.

There was a gate between the town of Woodstock and the park with a chamber over the gateway, janitor's house and stable. Several appointments to the office of gatekeeper are recorded in the thirteenth and fourteenth centuries: in 1267 the gatekeeper was allowed 2*d*. a day and half a mark a year for his robe.[82]

Early Extensions to the Park

In the early Middle Ages Woodstock Park quite clearly occupied a much more limited area than the present extent of Blenheim, and was confined to the western side of the Glyme valley, on land taken out of the township of Old Woodstock. It has grown to its present size by a series of additions, but as indicated above, the chronology and extent of the successive accretions is far from clear, and it has been difficult to reconcile the documentary sources either with each other or with the field evidence. Research for the Victoria County History of Oxfordshire (hereafter the V.C.H.), particularly work by Alan Crossley, Chris Day and Janet Cooper published in 1990,[83] has since done much to clarify the picture and is reflected in the following account:

    i. The extension of the park east of the Glyme, into the area known in the Middle Ages as Hensgrove and now as Lower

Park, was a result of an exchange of lands with the Knights Templars, probably made by Henry II when New Woodstock was laid out. Hensington lies in Bladon parish and, from 1256, references arise to the King's park at Bladon and to Bladon Gate in Hensgrove.[84] In 1575–6 the tenants of Woodstock manor referred to an earlier imparkment of the open fields of Hensington, in exchange for which the inhabitants of that hamlet were compensated by a grant of lands in Hordeley; the record in the Sandford Cartulary of a meadow near Stratford Bridge belonging to Hensington lends support to the view that this exchange had taken place before *c*. 1200.[85] The separate identity of Hensgrove was still being preserved in the late sixteenth century. Significantly this part of the park lay outside the legal bounds of Wychwood Forest: in 1609 the park within the Royal Forest west of the Glyme was said to contain 1,629 acres (*c*. 659 ha.), while the park outside the forest to the east was 452 acres (*c*. 183 ha.).[86] The Lower Park still contains a few dotard oaks which survive from the period before the ornamental plantations of the early eighteenth century.

ii. Evidence which may suggest another medieval extension to the north in the Great Park has been noticed in the area between the Column of Victory and the Fishery Cottage valley. In the winter of 1981–2 melting snow was seen to be lying in a series of gently curving bands on top of the plateau, and the pattern revealed bore a strong resemblance to that of ridge and furrow.[87] The amplitude of the ridging is so slight that under normal conditions it is virtually invisible. It is possible that this is a relic of some short-term ploughing campaign in the post-medieval period – it is known, for example, that many areas of normally permanent grassland and waste went under the plough during the emergency conditions of the Napoleonic War. The broad gauge of the ridging does, however, bear a greater resemblance to the forms usually associated with medieval open-field farming. It is possible, therefore, that the present contrast between the wooded High Park and the open plateau above the valley immediately to the north is not due solely to the eighteenth-century landscaping, but represents the incorporation of part of the open fields of Wootton parish within the park wall. Can this slight ridge and furrow really date from before the first enclosure of the park in the beginning of the twelfth century? Or does it represent a later medieval extension of the park over former arable land? In this context it is perhaps worth recalling that the fifteenth-century writer John Rous declared

42. Ridge and furrow in the Great Park, January 1982.

that many villages, churches and chapels had been swept away to make Woodstock Park. Rous had a particular axe to grind about contemporary evictions and enclosures, and was not above stretching his evidence to and beyond its limits;[88] however, his statement may be based on a genuine folk-memory of the extension of the park and the loss of farmland. The late Mrs V. Wickham Steed suggested that part of the original settlement of Old Woodstock had been destroyed in this process;[89] and though her evidence is not wholly convincing – some of the earthworks within the park wall here are undoubtedly ancient quarries, and molehills in this area have consistently refused to produce any medieval pottery – it is a possiblity which cannot be dismissed out of hand. Alan Crossley has recently reviewed the evidence for a northward enlargement of Henry I's park into Wootton parish. Commenting on the lack of specific later medieval evidence for this 'in an area well documented from the 12th century' he concludes that 'the whole northern park, not merely the section north of Akeman Street, may have been taken out of Wootton parish and . . . that the imparkment was very early.'[90]

Bibliography

BALLARD A. 1908: 'Woodstock Manor in the Thirteenth Century', *Vierteljahrschrift für Social-und Wirtschaftsgeschichte* Vol. 6, pp. 424–459.

BOND C.J. 1981: 'Woodstock Park under the Plantagenet Kings: the Exploitation and Use of Wood and Timber in a Medieval Deer Park', *Arboricultural Jnl.* Vol. 5, pp. 201–213.

BROWN R.A., COLVIN H.M. & TAYLOR A.J. 1963: *The History of the King's Works*, Vol. 2, *The Middle Ages* (H.M.S.O., London), pp. 1009–1017.

CHAMBERS E.K. 1936: *Sir Henry Lee: an Elizabethan Portrait* (Clarendon Press, Oxford).

CROSSLEY A. 1990: 'Blenheim', in *Victoria History of the County of Oxford*, vol. XII, pp. 430–470

MARSHALL E. 1873: *The Early History of Woodstock Manor and its Environs* (James Parker & Co., Oxford).

PLOT R. 1705: *The Natural History of Oxfordshire* (2nd edn., Oxford).

SCHUMER B. 1984: *The Evolution of Wychwood to 1400: Pioneers, Frontiers and Forests* (Leicester University Dept. of English Local History, Occasional Papers, 3rd ser. No. 6).

WOODWARD F. 1982: *Oxfordshire Parks* (Oxfordshire Museum Services Publication No. 16, Woodstock).

References and Footnotes

1   V.C.H. Oxon. I 1939, p. 401.

2   PLOT R. 1705, p. 357; STUBBS W. (Ed., 1913), *Select Charters and other illustrations of English Constitutional History* (9th edn., revised H.W.C. Davis, Oxford University Press), pp. 84–86.

3   COX J.C. 1905: *The Royal Forests of England* (Methuen, London); YOUNG C.R. 1979: *The Royal Forests of Medieval England* (Leicester University Press).

4   HAYDON F.S. (Ed.) 1858–63: *Eulogium (Historiarum sive Temporis)*, (Rolls Ser., Vol. 9), i, 269, iii, 297; ARNOLD T. (Ed.) 1879: *Henrici Archidiaconi Huntendunensis Historia Anglorum* (Rolls Ser., Vol. 74), p. 244.

5   WOODWARD F. 1982.

6   E.g. Calendar of Close Rolls (hereafter Cal. Close R.), 1231–4, 10; 1242–7, 226; 1261–4, 60, 328; 1268–72, 308, 340, 353, 466; 1279–82, 160, 213, 324, 329, 380; 1288–96, 172; Calendar of Liberate Rolls (hereafter Cal. Lib. R.), 1260–7, p. 146.

7   CHAMBERS E.K. 1936, p. 83.

8   Cal. Close R. 1302–7, 21.

9   E.g. Cal. Close R. 1256–9, 429; 1259–61, 110, 366; 1261–4, 8, 219; Cal. Lib. R. 1240–5, p. 263; 1251–60, p. 430; 1260–7, pp. 28, 42, 142, 155; 1267–72 Nos. 833, 857, 1808.

10 Cal. Close R. 1254–6, 245, 255; Cal. Lib. R. 1251–60, p. 272.

11 Cal. Close R. 1296–1302, 177.

12 Calendar of Patent Rolls (hereafter Cal. Pat. R.), 1441–6, p. 277; in addition to the deer from Woodstock Park, the same grant allowed Abingdon Abbey two bucks and a doe annually from the Forests of Stowood and Shotover, from Bernwood Forest, from Beckley Park and from Cornbury Park, also two bucks from Hampstead Marshall Park in Berkshire.

13 Cal. Close R. 1234–7, 400; 1237–42, 333–4; 1242–7, 227; 1259–61, 429; 1261–4, 68.

14 *Rotuli Liberate* (Record Commissioners), p. 43; Cal. Close R. 1279–88, 73; 1288–96, 467.

15 E.g. Cal. Close R. 1253–4, 42; 1259–61, 67, 79, 319, 320, 324; 1288–96, 300, 304, 349; Cal. Pat. R., 1343–5, 285; 1272–81, 215; 1292–1301, 61.

16 Cal. Close R. 1288–96, 432.

17 Cal. Close R. 1413–19, 175–6.

18 ROUS J. 1745: *Historia Reg. Angliae* (Ed. HEARNE T., Oxford), p. 138.

19 Cal. Close R. 1231–4, 63.

20 Cal. Lib. R. 1245–51, pp. 290, 364.

21   ILLINGWORTH W. Ed., 1818: *Rotuli Hundredorum temp. Hen. III & Edw. I in Turr' Lond'* (Record Commissioners), p. 41.
22   E.g. Cal. Close R. 1256–9, 144; 1307–13, 26, 191, 484; Calendar of Fine Rolls, (hereafter Cal. Fine R.) IV, 409; Cal. Lib. R. 1251–60, p. 455; 1260–67, pp. 154, 237; 1267–72, No. 121.
23   MIDGLEY L.M. Ed., 1942: *Ministers' Accounts of the Earldom of Cornwall, 1296–1297*, Vol. 1, Camden Soc. 3rd ser., Vol. 66, pp. 139–40; V.C.H. Oxon. VI 1959 p. 244, quoting P.R.O. C145/108/2; Cal. Close R. 1337–9, 220.
24   Wm. Salt Arch. Soc. Vol. V, reproduced in COX J.C. 1905: *The Royal Forests of England* (Methuen, London), Plate XXIV.
25   Cal. Close R. 1251–3, 2; Cal. Lib. R. 1251–60, p. 3.
26   Cal. Close R. 1254–6, 325.
27   Cal. Close R. 1296–1302, 440.
28   Cal. Close R. 1247–51, 285; *Testa de Nevill: Book of Fees* Pt. i (H.M.S.O., 1920), p. 103.
29   E.g. Cal. Close R. 1279–88, 516; 1318–23, 60; 1333–7, 266; 1360–4, 3; Cal. Fine R. IV, 409; Calendar of Inquisitions Miscellaneous II, 1307–49, No. 1958; Calendar of Memoranda Rolls 1326–7, No. 2179; Cal. Pat. R. 1345–8, 28; 1307–13, 554, 562; 1318–23, 60.
30   Cal. Close R. 1323–7, 390; Cal. Lib. R. 1251–60, p. 175.
31   Cal. Fine R. IV, 409.
32   Cal. Fine R. VII, 134.
33   BALLARD A. 1908, pp. 440, 442–3, 445–7.
34   MARSHALL E. 1873, p. 82; BALLARD A. 1908, 447.
35   Cal. Close R. 1247–51, 460; 1259–61, 48; Cal. Pat. R. 1247–58, 87, 570.
36   Cal. Pat. R. 1494–1509, 241.
37   CHAMBERS E.K. 1936, p. 82.
38   Cal. Close R. 1259–61, 363.
39   STUBBS W. (Ed.), 1889: *Willelmi Malmesbiriensis Monachi, de Gestis Regum Anglorum* (Rolls Ser., Vol. 90), ii, 485.
40   Cal. Lib. R. 1226–40, pp. 28, 30. For fuller discussion of local fishponds and their place in the medieval economy, see BOND C.J. & CHAMBERS R.A. 1988: 'Oxfordshire Fishponds,' in ASTON M.A. (Ed.): *Medieval Fisheries and Fishponds* (British Archaeological Reports, Oxford), 353–70.
41   Cal. Lib. R. 1240–5, p. 164.
42   Cal. Lib. R. 1251–60, p. 25.
43   Cal. Lib. R. 1251–60, p. 272.
44   CAMPBELL C. 1725: *Vitruvius Britannicus* Vol. III.
45   Cal. Close R. 1256–59, 397.
46   E.g. Cal. Close R. 1307–13, 26; Cal. Lib. R. 1226–40, pp. 28, 30, 177; 1245–51, 245; 1251–60, 86, 87, 165.
47   Cal. Close R. 1251–3, 167–8.
48   Cal. Close R. 1333–7, 243, 266.
49   Cal. Lib. R. 1240–5, p. 34; Cal. Close R. 1296–1302, 440; 1302–7, 188.
50   Cal. Close R. 1254–6, 433.
51   Cal. Close R. 1251–3, 336.
52   Cal. Lib. R. 1267–72, Nos. 1489, 1877.
53   Cal. Lib. R. 1267–72, No. 2026.
54   Cal. Close R. 1247–51, 426.
55   Calendar of Chancery Warrants Vol. 1, 1244–1326, p. 92.
56   Survey by BOND C.J. & STEANE J.M.: *Medieval Archaeology* Vol. 21 (1977), pp. 260–2.
57   Cal. Close R. 1333–7, 243.
58   MARSHALL E. 1873, p. 82; BALLARD A. 1908, p. 446.
59   ILLINGWORTH W. (Ed.), 1818 *Rotuli Hundredorum* (Record Commissioners), ii, p. 851; BALLARD A. 1908, p. 433; Cal. Fine R. Vol. VIII, p. 35.
60   1551 Inquisition of 'The Auntient Demeanes of the Mannor of Woodstock,' British Library (hereafter B.L.) Lansd. MS. No. 758; a copy made by Dr. Mavor and preserved by Vernon Watney

in the library at Cornbury was transcribed by Mrs V. Wickham Steed (Wickham Steed MSS, Oxon. County Museum, 2.1.19, pp. 579–587.

61 See BOND C.J. 1981 for a fuller discussion.

62 Cal. Fine R. Vol. I, p. 42; Cal. Close R. 1272–79, 205, 207, 369.

63 Cal. Close R. 1231–4, 16; 1268–72, 527; 1279–88, 216.

64 Cal. Close R. 1254–6, 279, 432–3; SALMAN L.F. 1967: *Building in England down to 1540* (Oxford University Press, 2nd edn.), pp. 228, 234.

65 Cal. Close R. 1264–8, 5.

66 ILLINGWORTH W. (Ed.), 1818: *Rotuli Hundredorum* (Record Commissioners), ii, p. 851.

67 Cal. Close R. 1231–4, 16; 1254–6, 432–3.

68 Cal. Close R. 1272–9, 207, 297, 312, 370, 372.

69 ILLINGWORTH W. (Ed.), 1818: *Rotuli Hundredorum* (Record Commissioners), ii, p. 851; Cal. Fine R. Vol. VIII, p. 35; BALLARD A. 1908, pp. 433, 436.

70 1551 Inquisition, see Ref. 60 above.

71 Cal. Close R. 1272–9, 192, 205, 207, 274, 283, 292, 306, 309, 312, 369, 370, 372; Cal. Fine R. Vol. I, pp. 41–2, 51.

72 For full details and references for the palace buildings, see BROWN R.A., COLVIN H.M. & TAYLOR A.J. 1963, pp. 1009–1017.

73 Cal. Lib. R. 1240–5, p. 164; Cal. Close R. 1333–7, 243, 266. CROSSLEY, A. 1990, p. 437 n., refutes earlier suggestions that this southern causeway was continued by a road leading south-eastwards across the park towards Oxford.

74 Pipe R. 12 Henry II, p. 116.

75 MARSHALL E. 1873, pp. 49–57.

76 Cal. Lib. R. 1226–40, p. 412; 1260–7, p. 154.

77 BROWN R.A., COLVIN H.M. & TAYLOR A.J. 1963, pp. 1015–6.

78 Aubrey's plan (Bodl. Lib. MS. Wood 276b, f.43v) is reproduced in BROWN R.A., COLVIN H.M. & TAYLOR A.J. 1963, plate 52, and the Gothic bathing-house design appears in GREEN D. 1951: *Blenheim Palace*, p. 207. I am grateful to John Campbell, who first drew my attention to the pitched stonework beneath the lake shore.

79 CROSSLEY, A. 1990, p. 438.

80 Cal. Close R. 1337–9, 220.

81 Cal. Close R. 1461–8, 41–2; the 1577 record (B.L. Lansdowne MS XXV., f. 191) is given in MARSHALL E. 1873, p. 160. See CROSSLEY, A. 1990, pp. 447–8. The original High Lodge was demolished in the Civil War. The name was transferred to the site of Straights Lodge by the early eighteenth century.

82 Cal. Pat. R. 1266–72, 92; 1361–4, 192. See CROSSLEY, A. 1990, p. 444.

83 I am especially grateful to Dr. Janet Cooper, until recently of the Oxfordshire staff of the Victoria County History, for her views on the extension of the park and for a number of the references which follow. Her recent work has called the traditional views of the park's successive expansions into question, and as a result I have made a number of corrections and amendments to my first draft. Dr. Cooper may still not be fully in agreement with my treatment of the evidence here, but any errors due to misunderstandings of the documentary sources are mine alone.

84 WATNEY V.J. 1910: *Cornbury and the Forest of Wychwood* (London), p. 218, quoting an Inquisition of 1219 (Public Record Office (hereafter P.R.O.), Chan. Misc. bdle 11, file 1, No. 19); see also MARSHALL E. 1873, pp. 30–48; and YOUNG C. 1979: *The Royal Forests of England*, p. 20.

85 B.L. Lansdowne MS. 27, f. 189v; LEYS A.M. (Ed.) 1940 *The Sandford Cartulary*, Vol. II Oxfordshire Record Society, Vol. 22, pp. 272–3.

86 1609 Survey of Wychwood Forest, P.R.O. LR. 2/202, ff. 25–50.

87 I am grateful to James Riley, who first called my attention to this.

88 ROUS J. (Ed. HEARNE T.) 1745: *Historia Reg. Angliae* (Oxford), p. 138. Rous's list of deserted villages in Warwickshire is widely known and justly valued as a near-contemporary record of later medieval settlement depopulation, but even this needs to be used with some caution (*cf.* BOND

C.J. 1982, 'Deserted Medieval Villages in Warwickshire and Worcestershire,' in SLATER T. & JARVIS P. (Eds.), *Field & Forest: an Historical Geography of Warwickshire and Worcestershire* (Geo Books, Norwich), esp. pp. 150–2).

89   Wickham Steed MSS 2.1.3, p. 29 (Oxfordshire County Museum).

90   CROSSLEY, A. 1990, p. 443.

5. WOODSTOCK PARK IN THE SIXTEENTH AND SEVENTEENTH CENTURIES

James Bond

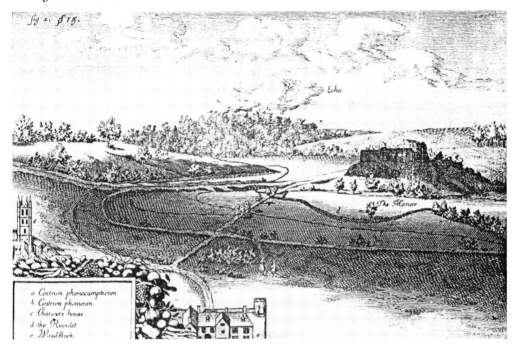

a *Centrum phonocampticum*
b *Centrum phonicum*.
c *Chaucers house*.
d *the Rivulet*
e *Woodstock*

The Destruction of the Royal Palace

THERE ARE signs that, by the early sixteenth century, Woodstock Palace was beginning to fall into decay. A survey of 1551 says that 'the mansion ... for many years past hath been decayed and prostrated.'[1] The gatehouse survived in sufficiently good condition to serve as accommodation for Princess Elizabeth during her internment following Sir Thomas Wyatt's rebellion in 1554, though some repairs to the 'tyling and glasyng' had to be carried out first.[2] It was again temporarily patched up to accommodate James I in 1603, and he returned on several occasions, attracted by the hunting. Charles I sometimes visited Woodstock, and there is a full description of the court, gatehouse, great hall, chapel and chambers in 1634, by which time a tennis-court had been built on the eastern side of the palace.[3] The palace was garrisoned during the Civil War, and on 17 April 1646 it was bombarded by Rainsborough's ordnance; a further attack followed on 24 April and two days later the Royalist garrison surrendered.[4]

After the execution of the king Parliament ordered a survey to be made of the palace and park, and this gives some interesting

43. The ruins of Woodstock Palace as illustrated by Dr. Robert Plot, 1677.

details of the structures then standing: the gatehouse gave access to a courtyard, on the north side of which was a range known as the Prince's lodgings, with the great hall to the east; adjoining this was a chapel, the Bishop's lodgings and the wardrobe court, surrounded by the Lord Chamberlain's lodgings and wardrobe rooms; beyond this was the Queen's hall and the steward's lodgings; a staircase led up to the guard-chamber, which adjoined the presence chamber and privy chamber, with the King's withdrawing-room, bed-chamber and closet on one side and the Queen's lodgings on the other; the privy garden, twenty perches in extent, surrounded by further buildings, and the pastry court surrounded by two large kitchens and other ranges; it was concluded that 'the saide house is much out of repair, yett most of it is fitter to stand than to be demolished'; the value of the timber, stone, brick, glass and iron was reckoned at £1,000.[5] The premises were purchased by Lt.-Gen. Fleetwood, and in 1651 were emptied of their remaining furniture and partly dismantled. The earliest known depiction of the house, made by Daniel King in 1665, suggests that it was still quite imposing, but the next view shows the palace in 1714 on the verge of ruin. The damage it had suffered during the Civil War and its aftermath had rendered it unsuitable for rehabilitation as a royal residence.[6]

The ruins of the palace survived into the 1720s. Sir John Vanbrugh was very anxious that what remained should be kept, and in 1709 he drew up a document entitled 'Reasons Offer'd for Preserving Some Part of the Old Manor', which must be amongst the earliest of all pleas for the preservation of a medieval monument. Indeed, he succeeded in thwarting the first Duchess's wish to have the ruins swept away for a number of years, living in the more inhabitable quarters for part of the time when he was working on Blenheim. The story is related that, whenever he saw the Duchess approaching, he hastily diverted his workmen to making a great show of demolishing relatively unimportant outbuildings, but as soon as she had gone he had them turn back to work on patching up the main buildings again. However, he could not succeed in this stratagem indefinitely, and when he was dismissed from Blenheim in 1716, the fate of the palace ruins was sealed. The last remnants were pulled down in 1723.[7]

Post-Medieval Extensions to the Park

A further substantial extension occurred in July 1576, when £309 was allocated for building a wall to enclose certain

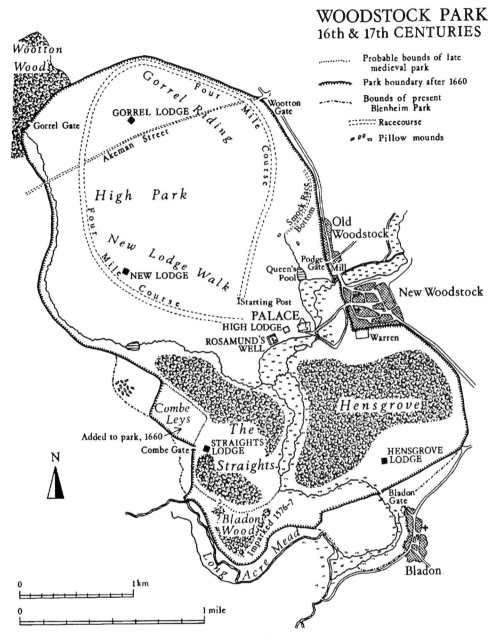

WOODSTOCK PARK
16th & 17th CENTURIES

.... Probable bounds of late medieval park
~~~~~~ Park boundary after 1660
–··–··– Bounds of present Blenheim Park
::::::::: Racecourse
◦ ๏๏ ◦ Pillow mounds

44.   Woodstock Park in the sixteenth and seventeenth centuries.

additions to Woodstock Park.[8] The tenants of Woodstock manor, aggrieved about the enclosure of their common and the diversion of a highway, took their complaint to the Queen at Windsor. The reply put them firmly in their place. The Queen directed the Master of the Requests to tell them how little cause they had to be aggrieved, and that she was much offended that such unthankful and unnatural subjects should find her actions a cause for complaint. Not content with this, some forty or fifty commoners made a further presentation of their case the following day, whereupon the Queen, very greatly annoyed, commanded them to depart or be punished: 'Surely it is not to be suffered that a Prince in such a case should be grudged at, when every upstart and yeoman almost can have more than a thousand times at their tenants' hands to enclose, whole towns and lordships, and to change twice as far highways, and no complaints at all of it.' Nonetheless, she commanded Lord Burghley to hear and deal with their complaints.[9] In July 1579 George Whitton, comptroller of the manor of Woodstock, was recompensed for certain grounds and meadows held by him on lease which had been resumed into the Queen's hands for the better feeding of her deer.[10]

The traditional interpretation of this extension, based upon the printed Calendars and followed by several earlier accounts, is that it involved an expansion to the north of the old park, including the blocking-up of the Akeman Street as a public road and its replacement by the road which now passes by the exterior of the Ditchley Gate. However, recent re-examination of the evidence by the Oxfordshire V.C.H. staff has shown that the park had already reached its present northern bounds by the Middle Ages, and has demonstrated beyond question that the extension recorded in 1576–7 took place in the south-western sector of the park.[11] The account roll for that year records that Sir Henry Lee built a stone wall eight feet high round 'the Straights within the park of Woodstock, Heynes Close, Bladon Wood and other grounds' for the preservation of red deer.[12] Lee's new enclosure was called Queen's Park. The Straights Walk is located by the 1650 Parliamentary Survey, comprising an area 254 acres, 2 roods and 11 poles in extent between the High Park on the north and Bladon Fields on the south.[13] Bladon Wood, which lay between Woodstock Park and Wychwood Forest in the 1240s, is not recorded by name after 1552,[14] and soon appears to have lost its separate identity within the extended park. The total length of the new wall built in 1576–7 was 355 poles, each pole being 24 feet long; this works out at around one and a half miles, which is just about the distance from the northern tip of Long Acre round to the Glyme. The original document amongst the Marquess of Salisbury's manuscripts referring to protests over changes in the highway unfortunately neither specifies which particular highway was blocked, nor lists the names of the protestors, which might have identified them as Bladon men. However, there is nothing to indicate that there was more than one extension to the park in 1576, and the material in the Public Record Office makes it quite clear that this was in the south-west.

Further works on the park wall are recorded in 1621–33 when John Whitton, comptroller and surveyor of the king's works, spent £340 on a wall separating the meadows from the lower ground (clearly shown on the sketch map of *c.* 1710) and again, perhaps more significantly, in 1635–7, when Whitton was charged with the task of enclosing a large area with a wall 8 feet high which, along with other works carried out at the same time, cost £1,710. The latter occasion sounds like a major operation, but it cannot relate to a new extension of the park north of Akeman Street, since there is already documentation for the building of Gorrel Lodge in 1572–3, and one of the brass plaques at Ditchley commemorating James I's hunting successes confirms that 'Goreil Gate' was in existence by 1608.[15] It must be remembered that walls did not only form the external boundaries

45. The park boundary north of Mapleton Pond. The present boundary follows the left-hand edge of the woodland. Another boundary appears as a cropmark inside the park to the right. It now seems likely that this marks the original inner boundary of the perimeter screen of trees, rather than an earlier park boundary as previously thought. The straight line across the centre of the photograph is Akeman Street.

1608 August 26 : Munday

RIDING
KING IAMES MADE ME TO RVN; FOR LIFE FROM DEADMANS
I RAN TO GOREIL GATE, WHERE DEATH FOR ME WAS BIDING

1610 August 25 Saturfday

FELL
FROM FOXEHOLE DRIVEN, WHAT COVLD I DOE; BEING LAME I
BEFORE THE KING & PRINCE; NERE ROZAMOND; HER WELL

46. Brass plaques at Ditchley commemorating King James I's hunting exploits in Woodstock Park.

of the park, but also some internal divisions within it, to keep the deer out of the meadowland for example.[16]

Aerial photographs of the north-western quarter of the park beyond Mapleton Pond show a long, curving linear mark across the arable land, the course of which is continued as a bank and ditch along the inner edge of the woodland screen.[17] In wet weather water sometimes collects along this line although it does not precisely coincide with the valley bottom. At the point where Akeman Street passes through this feature on the western side two small dots on one photograph suggest that gate-piers were once positioned here. At first this was tentatively interpreted as the line of the late sixteenth- or seventeenth-century park wall, implying a later extension out to the present boundary, but it now seems more likely merely to represent the original inner edge of Capability Brown's perimeter belt of trees.

The last documented addition to the park before its acquisition by the first Duke of Marlborough occurred in 1660, when a small area of furzy ground was taken in from Combe Green. On 25 February 1662 Sir William Fleetwood and William Morton certified that the expense of purchasing this furze land would be £616, to include £80 for building a new wall and £50 for compensating the poor tenants for the loss of their common; and on 7 March this payment was authorised.[18]

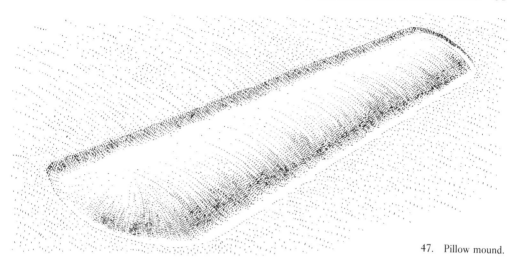

47.   Pillow mound.

Two later additions to the park occurred after its acquisition by the Marlboroughs. First, the area called the Lince, north of Bladon village, was imparked after the enclosure of the parish in 1767.[19] Second, in *c.* 1780, part of Old Assart Furlong in Combe became the rectangular embanked area now known as New Park. The reason for this latter small extension may be indicated by the earthworks within it: towards its northern end there is a series of a dozen pillow-mounds, the biggest concentration so far recognised anywhere in Oxfordshire. While the date and purpose of pillow-mounds remains somewhat open to question, it has been demonstrated that many of them are associated with the breeding of rabbits in the early post-medieval period, and this may, in fact, represent a large artificial rabbit-warren. It was not, however, the only part of the park where rabbits had been

48.   Pillow mound overlying the medieval park boundary, south of Icehouse Clump.

49.   Pillow mound north of Icehouse Clump.

introduced. At least two other isolated pillow-mounds can tentatively be identified, one to the north of the Icehouse Clump and another to the south, the second of which is clearly built over the top of the postulated north-eastern section of the park boundary referred to earlier; in 1649 it is recorded that thieves poaching in the coney-burrows behind Rosamund's Well were disturbed and fled in such haste that they left their ferret behind![20]

The Decline of the Park

By the later seventeenth century the park woodland appears to have been derelict and neglected. On 17 May 1660 Parliament ordered a cessation to the cutting down and despoliation of royal woods, but at Woodstock it was recorded that 'some persons, on pretext of orders from Sir Arthur Hasslerigg and Mr Fleetwood, assume the liberty of despoiling the timber and grazing the meadows there.' A warrant was issued 'to seize and stay all timber cut down or stacked, grass, or other products of Woodstock Park and Manor'.[21]

Woodstock Park had always been primarily a hunting-preserve, and the tide of fashion had now moved away from this preoccupation. The whole function of parks elsewhere was changing, as they came to fulfil a much wider range of ornamental and recreational functions. For the moment, with the decline of the palace, there was little incentive to exploit the ornamental potential of the site; but new forms of recreation and amusement were already beginning to make their appearance. Sir Arthur Haslerig, who held the park during the interregnum, maintained there the bloodstock which he had acquired partly from the dispersal of the royal stud at Tetbury; the sale of his bloodstock is recorded in an advertisement in *Mercurius Politicus* on 20/27 October 1659. Lord Lovelace, who took up residence in the gatehouse of the half-ruined royal palace after the Restoration, was a keen sportsman and patron of the turf, and he promoted a series of race-meetings in the park, first recorded in 1676. Woodstock thus became the third oldest race-meeting in Oxfordshire, following the institution of horse-races at Burford (1620) and Oxford (1630). Brief details of many of the early meetings appear in the diary of Arthur Annesley, 3rd Earl of Anglesey (d.1686), whose seat lay at nearby Bletchingdon, and Anthony Wood's diary records on 19 October 1679 a visit by Titus Oates to Lord Lovelace's meeting.

The early races had been run primarily for the benefit of the local gentry and their friends, but by 1681 the Woodstock meetings were sufficiently important to warrant attention from the metropolitan press, and reports regularly appeared in the *London Gazette* from 1681 to 1721. The meetings lasted for several days, usually in mid-September, but sometimes also in May or June. Lord Lovelace had initially provided a gold cup as a prize, and the main events were normally run for a plate valued at between £20 and £60; bucks and does from the park were also given as prizes for the subsidiary races during the early years. The *London Gazette* in 1684 records a race around the 'Four Mile Course' in the park, and this is shown on the earliest known sketch-plan of Blenheim, dated to *c*.1710. The starting-point was on the high plateau north-west of the old palace, dropping into the two dry valleys beyond on its way towards the Wootton Gate, then curving round the inside of the east and north walls of the park on flat, even ground; from the northern bounds of the park, the course swung round south-westwards across flat, easy country, with a slight dip and then a final slightly downhill dash to the finish and judge's seat. From 1677 foot-races or smock-races were also introduced, being held on the last day of the race-meetings. These were run on a separate course, also shown on the map of *c*.1710, starting just north-east of Queen Pool and continuing up the dry valley which, in the nineteenth century, was still known as Smock Race Bottom. After Lovelace's death in 1693 the Woodstock races continued for a few years under the patronage of Lord Abingdon of Rycote, with a brief intermission from 1699 to 1702. When the park came into the hands of the Marlboroughs, the first Duke and Duchess continued to support the meeting, providing a £50 gold plate in 1705.

The landscaping of the park, to be discussed in the next chapter, does not seem to have affected the race-course: although the plan of *c*.1710 shows Wise's Grand Avenue intersecting it, the

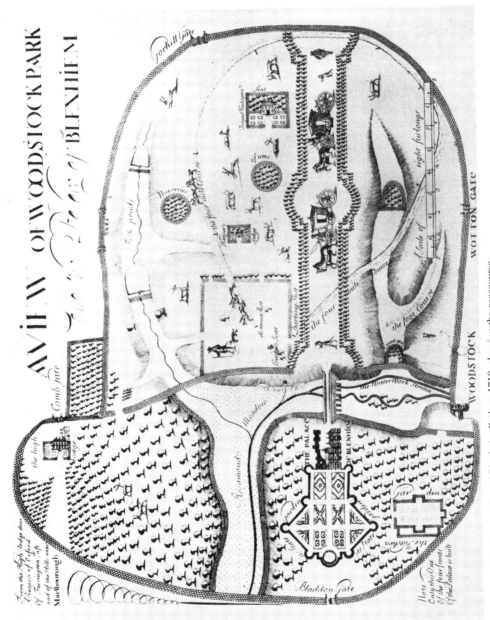

50.   The earliest known plan of Blenheim Park, *c.* 1710, showing the racecourse.

Vitruvius Britannicus plan of 1725 shows quite clearly that a gap in the trees was left to accommodate its passage. Such a gap would, of course, have made little difference to the apparent continuity of the avenue when viewed from the new Palace or from the Ditchley Gate. The death of the first Duke of Marlborough was to mark the suspension of racing in the park for a decade, and there were only two brief revivals subsequently. In 1732 John Cheny's *Historical List of all the Horse-Matches run in England and Wales* (1727–49) records a purse of 50 guineas provided by the Duchess, but the races seem to have lapsed again after June 1734. Finally, around 1810, Charles Richardson, the Combe antiquarian, records a two-mile course laid out in the park by the fourth Duke, 'but as it much disturbed the cattle, it was soon discontinued.'[22]

It would be dangerous to assume from the general absence of records of maintenance and the occasional record of despoliation that the park had fallen into a state of total decay during the course of the sixteenth and seventeenth centuries. There are strong indications, however, that the Crown had lost all interest in both park and palace by the last quarter of the seventeenth century; and although the grant of the property to the first Duke of Marlborough is usually portrayed as a gift of great munificence and generosity, the cynic could well argue that this was a convenient way of offloading a derelict royal estate which was not only surplus to requirements, but had also become a positive embarrassment.

The parcel of land which makes up Blenheim Park today, then, has a complex and fascinating history extending backwards in time for many centuries prior to the arrival of the Marlboroughs. Fragments of the landscape of these earlier periods still remain today, and more can be pieced together from the voluminous documentary sources; but there still remains much which is not yet fully understood, a challenge to future historians and archaeologists.

Bibliography

CHAMBERS E.K. 1936: *Sir Henry Lee: an Elizabethan Portrait* (Clarendon Press, Oxford).

COLVIN H.M., SUMMERSON J., BIDDLE M., HALE J.R. & MERRIMAN M. 1982: *The History of the King's Works*, Vol. 4, 1485–60 (part ii) (H.M.S.O., London), pp. 349–355.

CROSSLEY, A. 1990: 'Blenheim', in *Victoria History of the County of Oxford*, Vol. XII, pp. 430–70.

MARSHALL E. 1873: *The Early History of Woodstock Manor and its Environs* (James Parker & Co., Oxford).

References and Footnotes

1   B.L. Lansdowne MS No. 758, quoted in MARSHALL E. 1873, p. 150.

2   HAMILTON W.D. (Ed.), 1877: *A Chronicle of England by Chas. Wriothesley* (Camden Soc.), part ii, p. 116; MARSHALL E. 1873, p. 153.

3   B.L. Lansdowne MS 313, pp. 319–348, quoted in MARSHALL E. 1873, pp. 189–191. The provision of hasps and hinges for the 'tenys play gate' was recorded in 1528–9: COLVIN H.M., SUMMERSON J. *et al.* 1982, p. 351.

4   MARSHALL E. 1873, pp. 191–202.

5   P.R.O. Parliamentary Surveys: E. 317/Oxon,12, Fol.7, quoted in MARSHALL E. 1873, pp. 206–7; COLVIN H.M., SUMMERSON J. *et al.* 1982, pp. 354–5.

6   MARSHALL E. 1873, pp. 199–203; BALLARD A. 1896: *Chronicles of the Royal Borough of Woodstock* (Alden & Co., Oxford), p. 88.

7   Vanbrugh's plea is reproduced in GREEN D. 1951: *Blenheim Palace*, pp. 303–4. See also BREWER J. 1813: *Topography of Oxfordshire* (The Beauties of England & Wales, London), p.394.

8   Hist. MSS. Commission 1888: *Calendar of the MSS of the Most Hon. the Marquis of Salisbury preserved at Hatfield House, Herts.*, part ii (H.M.S.O., London), p. 135, No. 390.

9   B.L. Lansdowne MS 25, ff.189–99; 27, ff.95–6; 104, f.35; Hist. MSS. Comm. 1888, *Cal. of MSS of Marquis of Salisbury preserved at Hatfield House*, pt. ii, p. 141, No. 414.

10 Hist. MSS. Comm. 1888: *Cal. of MSS of Marquis of Salisbury preserved at Hatfield House*, pt. ii, p. 261, No. 742.

11 Eg. CHAMBERS E.K. 1936, pp. 92–4; Wickham Steed MSS. 2.1.20, p. 615 (Oxfordshire County Museum); BOND C.J. 1981, 'Woodstock Park under the Plantagenet Kings', *Aboricultural Jnl.* Vol. 5, p. 211. CROSSLEY A. 1990, pp. 441–3.

12 P.R.O. E 101/670/28; COLVIN H.M., SUMMERSON J. et al. 1982, p. 353.

13 P.R.O. E 317/12.

14 WATNEY V.J. 1910: *Cornbury and the Forest of Wychwood*, p. 220.

15 COLVIN H.M., SUMMERSON J. *et al.* 1982, p. 353. The inscriptions on the Ditchley plaques are quoted in MARSHALL E. 1873, p. 173.

16 CROSSLEY A. 1990, p. 443.

17 Fairey Aviation Surveys 6125/9.032 (24.6.1961).

18 Calendar of State Papers Domestic (hereafter Cal. S. P. Dom.), 1661–2, pp. 284, 302, 315, 503.

19 Wickham Steed MSS 2.1.20, p. 615 (Oxfordshire County Museum); Bladon Inclosure Award, Blenheim Muns.

20 Quoted in Alden's *Complete Guide to Blenheim & Woodstock* (Woodstock Town Council, 1924), p. 22; I am grateful to Ival Hornbrook for this reference, the original source for which I have not yet succeeded in locating. For a general description of rabbit farming and warren management, see SHEAIL J. 1971: *Rabbits and their History* (Newton Abbot).

21 Cal. S. P. Dom. 1660–1, p. 79.

22 The 1659 advertisement for the sale of Haslerig's bloodstock is quoted in HORE J.P. 1886: *History of Newmarket and Annals of the Turf*, Vol. ii, pp. 180–2. Annesley's diary is quoted in the same source, Vol. iii, pp. 131–2, 134, 137–9. Titus Oates's visit is recorded in CLARK A. (Ed.), 1892: *The Life and Times of Anthony Wood, Vol. ii, 1664–1681* (Oxford Historical Soc., Vol. XXI), p. 465. For the temporary transfer of Woodstock races to Oxford under Lovelace in 1680 and Lord Abingdon in 1706, see THOMPSON E.M. (Ed.), 1875: *Letters of Humphrey Prideaux to John Ellis, 1674–1722* (Camden Soc., Vol. CXX), pp. 97–8, and DOBLE C.E. (Ed.), 1885: *Remarks and Collections of Thomas Hearne, Vol. i* (Oxford Historical Soc., Vol. VI), p. 287. RICHARDSON C. 1823: *Collection of some Antiquities, Priveleges etc. of the Borough and Manor of New Woodstock*, is Bodleian Library MS. Top.Oxon. *c.* 351, f.217–8. I owe all the above references to Evelyn Brown-Grant, and I am most grateful to her for allowing me to make use of her notes on the Woodstock races in advance of her own publication.

6. BLENHEIM: THE PALACE AND GARDENS UNDER VANBRUGH, HAWKSMOOR AND WISE

David Green

ON 17 FEBRUARY 1705 Queen Anne announced to the House of Commons her intention of conferring upon John Churchill, 1st Duke of Marlborough, in recognition and gratitude for his services to the country during the war against the French, the 'honour and manor of Woodstock ... that demolished messuage, courthouse or toft ... called Woodstock Manor-House, and all that piece or parcel of ground commonly called ... Woodstock Park, ... containing in the whole by estimation 1,793 acres & 2 roods'.[1] Here, on the plateau above the River Glyme facing the medieval royal palace on the opposite bank a new, and even grander, palace was to arise, to be named Blenheim, after the site at Blindheim by the Nebel marshes in Bavaria where, six months earlier, Marlborough with Eugene had defeated the French army.[2]

The architect chosen for Blenheim was John Vanbrugh – at first sight a somewhat surprising choice, for he had no formal architectural training. John Vanbrugh had been born in Chester in 1664, the son of a wealthy confectioner, and grandson of Giles Van Brugg, a protestant merchant of Ghent who had fled to London to escape religious persecution. He joined the army, and in 1690 was arrested for spying on the fortifications of Calais; from early in 1691 to November 1692 he was held

51. Blenheim Palace, aerial view from the north.

52, 53. John and Sarah Churchill, First Duke and Duchess of Marlborough, portraits by Kneller.

prisoner in the Bastille, where, to pass the time, he began writing plays. He first made his reputation in the mid-1690s as the author of several popular comedies, best-known of which are *'The Provok'd Wife'* and *'The Relapse'*. However, drawing upon his knowledge of military architecture and his theatrical experience, he developed a genuine flair for design on the grand scale, and the Duke of Marlborough is known to have been very impressed with the model scheme for Castle Howard, which Vanbrugh had prepared for Charles Howard, 3rd Earl of Carlisle, in 1699, and declared that he wanted something similar at Blenheim. Vanbrugh was well aware of his own lack of the necessary practical experience to organise projects on this scale, and he had taken on as his assistant Nicholas Hawksmoor, who had years of practical training in the Office of Works. At Castle Howard Vanbrugh and Hawksmoor between them had brought a fair and splendid child into the world 'out of bushes, bogs and briars'.[3] Faced with the marshy chasm in Woodstock Park as they first saw it in the winter or early spring of 1704–5, Marlborough and Vanbrugh must indeed have shared courage and imagination on the Blenheim scale, for both recognised the capabilities (if I may be forgiven for anticipating a later chapter) of that wild and unmerciful site and were prepared to tackle them. Nothing short of a woman, who had courage aplenty but lacked vision, imagination or charity, could stop them from creating a castle (as it was then called) and a setting for it which

54. Sir John Vanbrugh, portrait attributed to Closterman; and Nicholas Hawksmoor, bust in the buttery of All Souls College, Oxford

should be altogether worthy of a great general and of a great and munificent queen.

Work began in June 1705. While Blenheim was being built, one of the thousand workmen was heard to complain of 'the enormity' of the work: having no bulldozers but only spades with which to dig out 13,040 'solid yards of earth' for the foundations, this must surely have been an understandable and heartfelt remark. The problems of design and construction were exacerbated by a background of personal bickering and political strife. In 1710 Duchess Sarah quarrelled with the Queen, the Tories came to power, and government funds dried up. By 1712 the original estimate had been overspent by £120,000 and the masons were suing the Duke for the £45,000 which they were owed. Work resumed in 1716 at the Marlboroughs' own expense, but the Duchess soon fell out with Vanbrugh, and he and Hawksmoor left Blenheim; when poor Vanbrugh returned in 1725 to view the completed palace, he was not even allowed admission into the park.[4]

Of Vanbrugh's problems with the building, and with the Duchess, there is, perhaps luckily, room to say little; the story is, in any case, familiar enough. Here we are more concerned with the setting of that building than with those responsible for the original plan. At that date, of course, it went without saying that, since a mansion must be manifestly man-made, formal and symmetrical, so too must its gardens, or at least those close to the house. If Nature were to be given her say at all, then it must be, in Vanbrugh's phrase, 'in places more solemn and retired'. For axial lines one had a compass; the main approaches and walks would be straight. There would be balance, and, in courts and gardens especially, much attention would be given to scale, the whole complex of the exterior being but a backdrop for the glorious beings who were to stroll there; or, if they chose, to look down from Hall or Saloon to the fountains and writhing arabesques of dwarf box leading to trimmed evergreens, to the park and pasture beyond, and just within sight beyond the margins of the park, the tower of Bladon church.

Even so, with an architect of Vanbrugh's originality, rules could, often with dramatic effect, be broken. He may have studied Palladio, but, like Wren and Hawksmoor, he was not to be dictated to in the matter of his own design. With the roofscape of the palace in particular, he would allow himself free rein, and as for the grounds, who could guess what he may have had up his sleeves for the main approach from the north, the *Pons Blenheimensis* (a bridge for those ghostly Roman legions who had known Akeman Street) and for the state garden on the

55.   Vanbrugh's original scheme for the south front of Blenheim.

56.   The south front as built, from *Vitruvius Britannicus* Vol. I, 1717.

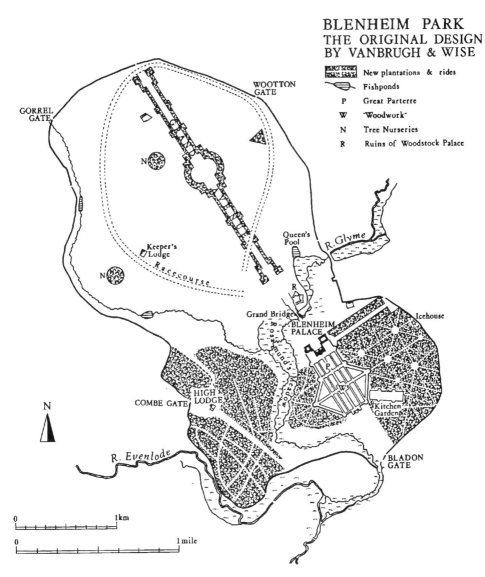

BLENHEIM PARK
THE ORIGINAL DESIGN
BY VANBRUGH & WISE

New plantations & rides
Fishponds
P Great Parterre
W "Woodwork"
N Tree Nurseries
R Ruins of Woodstock Palace

WOOTTON GATE

GORREL GATE

N

N

Keeper's Lodge

Racecourse

Queen's Pool

R.Glyme

R

Grand Bridge

Rosamond's Meadow

BLENHEIM PALACE

Icehouse

P

W

HIGH LODGE

COMBE GATE

Kitchen Garden

N

R. Evenlode

BLADON GATE

0   1km

0   1 mile

57. Blenheim Park: the design of John Vanbrugh and Henry Wise.

south? The garden which began to emerge was to occupy 77 acres, including a four-sided 250-yard parterre before the south-east front of the palace, patterned in dwarf box, sand and crushed brick, leading to a vast, six-sided, formal wilderness, to be called 'the Woodwork', containing shaped shrubs and clipped greens, centring upon two fountains. It was enclosed within a handsome stone wall, punctuated at each point where it changed direction by eight great round bastions, each 150 feet wide. It was known at the time as a military garden with curtain walls, and from those walls one could either look inwards, down upon Henry Wise's embroidery of graduated yews, hollies, bays and laurels, grown in his nurseries at Brompton Park, or out into Woodstock Park itself, which was now being formalised with radiating avenues and circles of limes and elms.

'The garden walls were set a-going,' we are told, 'the same day as the house', i.e. 18 June 1705;[5] and yet, two years later, as we now know, major changes were being introduced. Not only was the giant order of the garden front changed from Doric to Corinthian, but to east and west two large service courts were added (the stables court on the west was never completed). Feverish rebuilding ensued, and the Duchess, who had been busy at Court where she was, as Godolphin told Marlborough, 'of extremely prying-into habits', was only just in time to veto the third fountain and grotto planned for the southernmost extremity of the state garden, 750 yards from its beginning beyond the steps leading down from the saloon. She could not, however, stop them from finishing an eight-acre kitchen-

58. Henry Wise, portrait by Kneller.

garden, half a mile south-east of the house, with two round pools and four 100-foot bastions punctuating its fourteen-foot high brick walls.

Who, we must now ask, was responsible for the master-plan? Aside from the never-ending debate as to how much Vanbrugh and how much Hawksmoor was responsible for the palace itself, we are left with three candidates for the conception of the state or military garden: Marlbrough himself, Vanbrugh, and Queen Anne's master-gardener, Henry Wise.

'Who can be wise, amazed, temperate and furious, loyal and neutral in a moment? No man.' It was not in the mild nature of Henry Wise (1653–1738) to be furious. Almost alone in never falling out with the Duchess, he chose as his motto: 'Be ye wise as serpents and harmless as doves';[6] and indeed, as we look at his portrait by Kneller (Plate 58), the word that springs to mind is 'benign'. He was a family man of firmness and kindness, and at the same time was astute enough to make a fortune, laboriously earned. At the founding of Blenheim, as Laurence Whistler points out,[7] Wise's status was probably comparable with Vanbrugh's. Queen Anne liked and trusted him; and so did Marlborough. His contribution to the Blenheim gardens must have been considerable; but whether the overall concept can be attributed to him is doubtful. The ultimate inspiration would seem to be Vanbrugh's: thanks to his biographer, we have been made aware of Captain Vanbrugh's obsession with mock-fortification and, more especially, of his design for the outworks in the grounds of Castle Howard.

At one early stage Marlborough's impatience to enjoy a finished garden, expressed in his letters home from Flanders, grew so great that his Duchess, Sarah, directed all the masons then working on the palace (and they included the Strongs, Wren's chief masons for St Paul's Cathedral) to drop everything and divert their attention to the garden walls. They relaxed – working in the gardens was all so mechanical, so restful – and it was all that Sarah could do , once she realised her folly, to recall them to more exacting and intricate operations.

For her own garden on the east, to be looked down upon from the Bow Window Room and from her bedroom, the Duchess insisted upon box-edged beds in a setting of lavender and roses, jasmine and honeysuckle, pinks, rosemary and lilies. All these, and a great deal more, Wise caused to be sent down by West Country barge from his Brompton Nurseries, which then covered most of the ground now occupied by the South Kensington museums. But Blenheim, like its neighbours at Ditchley and Rousham, was never intended to be a flower-

59. Pool in the Blen-
heim kitchen-garden.

garden. For one thing, the scale was too vast. In the walled kitchen-garden Wise grew no less than twenty-eight different kinds of peach and nectarine, seventy-two kinds of pear, plums, figs, mulberries, apples, quinces and cherries. 'The kitchen garden, now the trees are in full vigour and full of fruit,' Vanbrugh assured the Duke, 'is really an astonishing sight. All that I ever saw in England or abroad of the kind are trifles to it.' The kitchen-garden walls, built of 500,000 bricks from Hanborough, with dressings of Taynton stone, still stand, with a Palladian gateway inserted into their western face by William Chambers in 1766–75; but the state garden lasted only fifty years before Lancelot Brown grassed it over (Chapter 8); yet even now, after drought, the ghost of the great parterre can be picked out on the lawn and the outline of the squares and quatrefoils of its beds can clearly be discerned from the air.

Beyond the kitchen-garden, out towards the eastern park wall, another feature completed during this first phase of activity was the icehouse. The Duke expressed a wish that this should be given priority during the long, hot summer of 1707. Built

60.   The icehouse at Blenheim.

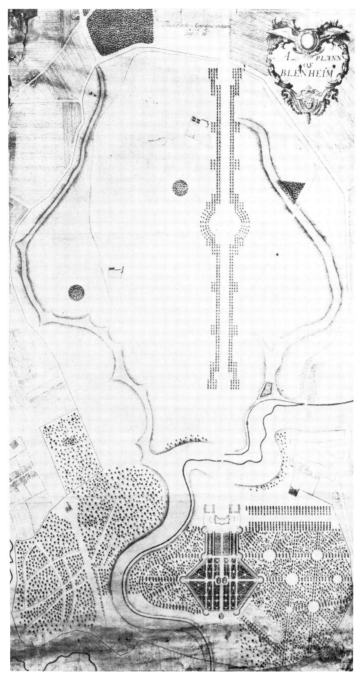

61.   Bridgman's plan of the park and garden at Blenheim made for Henry Wise in 1709.

probably to the design of Henry Wise, it consists of a mound 3m high and 20m in diameter, with a flat stone façade with a door (blocked since *c*.1950) giving entry to a large subterranean egg-shaped chamber. Ice was brought here in winter by waggon from the reservoirs near High Lodge and stored, packed between layers of insulating straw.[8]

One of the most valuable sources for the development of the park and gardens at this time is the large coloured plan which Charles Bridgman drew for Henry Wise, to whom he was then apprenticed, in 1709. Some thirty years ago Providence saw to it that I was able to divert this noble plan to the Great Hall at Blenheim, where it customarily hangs and surely belongs. Bridgman, important though he is in the history of the English garden, played a relatively small part at Blenheim (Sarah later engaged him for minor works, and, later still, quarrelled violently with his widow).

Bridgman's plan shows not only the gardens, but also the wider scheme for the park as a whole, with the Grand Avenue running north-west to the Ditchley Gate, where Hawksmoor had planned a gate which was never built; and the Mall, which was intended to be the main entrance from the Oxford road to the east. The approach from the north-west crossed the Glyme valley by the Grand Bridge, a truly monumental structure, with its main arch spanning 101 feet; Vanbrugh's original design for this followed the model of Palladio's bridges, with towers and arcades rising to a height of 80 feet. Stephen Switzer was briefly involved in the foundation of the bridge when construction began in 1708, and the masons Townsend and Peisley had completed the main arch by 1710; but two years later work

62. Vanbrugh's original design for the Grand Bridge, from *Vitruvius Britannicus* Vol. I, 1717.

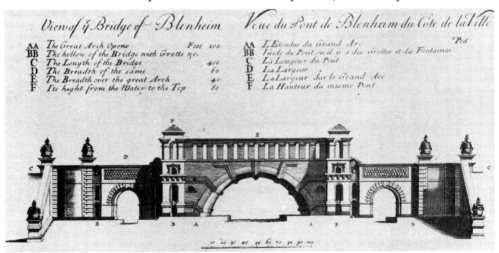

ground to a halt with the bridge uncompleted. If Vanbrugh had
created nothing else, it would surely stand as a great memorial to
a great architect. The Duchess, as was to be expected, mocked
at it as 'that bridge in the air,' a folly with thirty-three useless,
empty rooms; and even Marlborough had doubts as to whether
enough earth could ever be brought to join it to the sides of what
was still a chasm; and it was a strange irony that the bridge could
only become serviceable when, in the face of all Vanbrugh's
protests, what was left of Woodstock Manor had been demolished; some of its ruined walls were quarried to provide parts of
the bridge with a rubble filling, and the very hill upon which it
stood was reduced to provide material to fill those gaps at the
valley side and to create a high causeway.

Sarah saw to it that the bridge was never to carry the arcaded
superstructure which Vanbrugh had intended. In the gardens,
too, she vetoed the western orangery (balancing that on the
east), which, as Vanbrugh was at pains to explain, he had
intended as a room to rest in at sunset, and not, decidedly not,
'for a parcel of foolish plants'.

Before Vanbrugh left Blenheim in 1716 he had approved the
elm avenues to north and east, and the planting of the Grand
Avenue, with 686 large elms costing 2s.6d. each, was begun. At
the Duke's request Wise transplanted full-grown trees in
baskets, so that it appeared as if they had stood there for thirty or
forty years. Two double rows of English Elms (*Ulmus procera/
Ulmus campestris*) formed the main avenue, with a battlemented
plan formed by the addition of short blocks, each four trees long

63. Hawksmoor's
unused design for the
garden bridge.

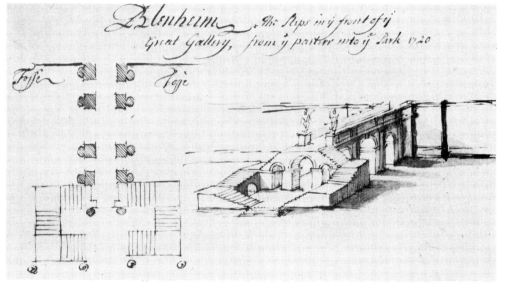

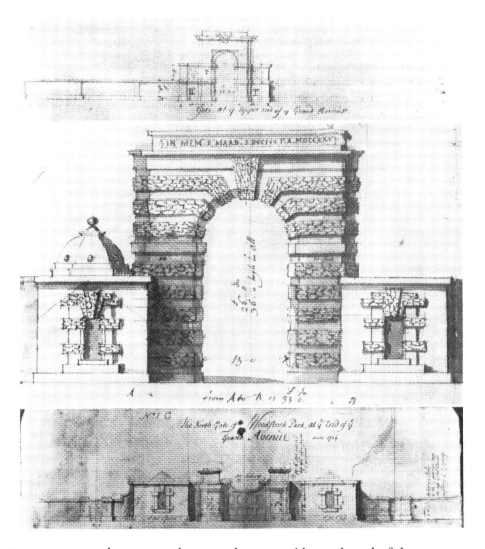

64–66. Hawksmoor's alternative designs for the Ditchley Gate.

and two trees deep, on the outer side; each end of the avenue was staggered outwards, terminating in paired blocks of eight trees, and in the centre of the avenue was an elliptical feature outlined by two rows of four trees.[9] Vanbrugh had also proposed a grotto under the Long Library at ground level, while Hawksmoor drew sketch after sketch for obelisks and other garden features, and, again, for the west front, an elaborate garden-bridge. Nothing came of any of these designs, and when Sarah took over following Marlborough's incapacity through a stroke in 1716, she declared: ''tis a chaos which only God Almighty could finish.' She did her best, and worst, to finish it.

67. The eastern elm avenue, looking towards the palace, photograph by Henry Taunt, 1883.

Bibliography

ANTHONY J. 1977: *Vanbrugh: an Illustrated Life of Sir John Vanbrugh, 1664–1726* (Shire Lifelines No.42, Princes Risborough).

DOWNES K. 1969: *Hawksmoor* (Thames & Hudson, London).

GREEN D. 1951: *Blenheim Palace* (Country Life, London), Chs. III–XIV, pp. 37–143.

GREEN D. 1956: *Gardener to Queen Anne: Henry Wise (1653–1738) and the Formal Garden* (Oxford University Press).

LEES-MILNE J. 1970: *English Country Houses, Baroque, 1685–1715* (Country Life, London).

WHISTLER L. 1938: *Sir John Vanbrugh, Architect and Dramatist, 1664–1726* (Cobden-Sanderson).

WHISTLER L. 1954: *The Imagination of Vanbrugh and his Fellow Artists* (Batsford, London).

References

1   Act, 3 & 4 Anne c. iv (al 6): *Statutes of the Realm*, Vol. VIII (London, 1821), p. 338.

2   An account of the Battle of Blenheim is given in GREEN D. 1974: *Blenheim* (Collins, London).

3   WEBB G. (Ed.): *The Complete Works of Sir John Vanbrugh*, Vol. IV, *The Letters* (Nonesuch edn.), p. 5.

4   GREEN D. 1951; MARSHALL E. 1873: *The Early History of Woodstock Manor* (James Parker & Co., Oxford), pp. 262–3.

5   Blenheim Muns. A.I.27.

6   St. Matthew Ch.10 v.16.

7   WHISTLER L. 1954.

8   For further information on icehouses in general, see, e.g., YORKE F.W.B. 1954: 'Some Midland Ice-houses', *Transactions of Birmingham Archaeological Society* Vol. 72, pp. 18–27; ELLIS M. 1982: *Ice and Icehouses through the Ages, with a gazetteer for Hampshire* (Southampton University Industrial Archaeology Group).

9   GREIG B.J.W. 1981: 'The History of the Elm Avenues at Blenheim and Dutch Elm Disease', *Quarterly Journal of Forestry* Vol. LXXV No.4, esp. pp. 207–8.

7. BLENHEIM AFTER VANBRUGH: THE SECOND PHASE

David Green & James Bond

VANBRUGH, building as usual from east to west, had all but finished the private apartments and central block of Blenheim Palace by the time of his departure, and the Marlboroughs finally moved in in 1719.

In 1722 Marlborough died at Windsor Lodge, and in 1723 the proud Duke of Somerset, whilst remodelling Petworth House in Sussex (tantalisingly, he does not record the name of his architect, now thought to be Daniel Marot), had the effrontery to propose to Marlborough's widow. Her refusal was not as harsh as Horace Walpole would have us suppose. In fact she wrote quite charmingly; but she did say 'if I know anything of myself I would not marry the Emperor of the World tho' I were but thirty years old.' They continued to write to each other, and she valued his advice.

One of the least satisfactory aspects of the original design was the discord between the grand formal approach from the north-west with Vanbrugh's magnificent bridge soaring over the insignificant and wayward River Glyme. The Duchess was determined to do something about this, and she told in a letter to the Duke of Somerset how she had called in Colonel Armstrong, who had been Marlborough's chief engineer. The scheme which he devised, and which was executed by the masons William Townsend and Bartholomew Peisley Jr. in the mid-1720s, is shown overdrawn on a rough plan of 1719:[1] the Glyme was to be dammed at the crossing-point of the lower causeway to the old manor and its waters were to be fed down over a cascade of twelve steps into a straight canal, 1,840 feet (560m) long and 100 feet (30m) broad, which was to pass under the central arch of the Grand Bridge and was to terminate in 'a Circuler Basin of 300 feet [90m] Diameter.'[2] On either side of the main central canal parallel narrower channels were to pass through the side arches of the bridge, carrying off surplus water and supplying Aldersea's ingenious pumping engine which lifted water from Rosamund's Well up to the cistern above the East Gate of the Palace.[3] On the Woodstock side, above the cascade, 'There is to be a lake . . .' wrote Sarah, and continued smugly, 'Sir John never thought of this cascade, which will be the finest and largest that ever was made, and the water constantly will flow from it without any trouble' (though Hawksmoor told Lord Carlisle in 1731 that 'The lake is beautiful, but the cascade does not play'). 'The fine green

68, 69.   Boydell's engravings of Col. Armstrong's formal canal scheme, published in 1752.

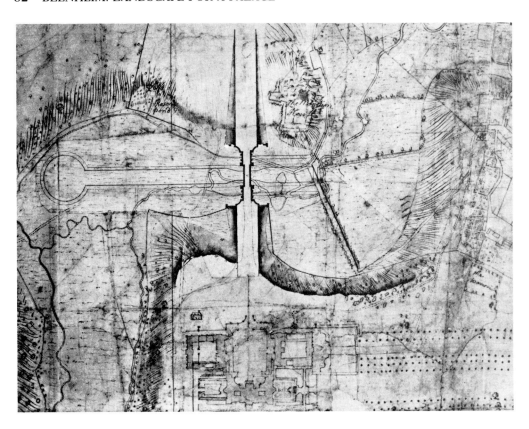

70.   The design for the formal canal and basin, as added to the 1719 plan.

meadow . . .' (to continue quoting Sarah) '. . . between the house and the wood is to remain as it is, and I believe your Grace will think in that, Nature cannot be mended; tho' Sir John formerly set his heart in turning that into a lake, as I will do it on the other side; and I will have swans and all such sort of things . . ..' At Rosamund's Bower, she adds, 'I will have something like those temples which they talk of which are at my lord Burlington's country house'.

Apart from the amended 1719 plan mentioned above, three prospects of the canal scheme are known, two of which (one from the town side and one from below the round pond, made by Boydell in 1752) show the scheme in idealised form. The third view is a painting made after Sarah's death in 1744, which seems to show Nature already beginning to blur with grass and weeds the straight edges of Armstrong's rather boring canal.[4] Despite this illustrative material, doubt has been expressed on some occasions whether Armstrong's canal ever progressed beyond the drawing-board.

In the mid-1970s a large collection of vertical air photographs

making up a near-complete coverage of Oxfordshire, commissioned in 1961 by the County Council from Fairey Aviation
Surveys, was deposited with the Sites & Monuments Record in
the County Museum at Woodstock. When the Blenheim coverage was examined it transpired that the canal and round basin
had indeed been built, and were dramatically revealed, showing
up clearly beneath the waters of Lancelot Brown's lake.[5]
Moreover, the photographs revealed an additional feature not
shown on the Townsend & Peisley plan, a pair of light parallel
lines joining the round pond, taking off south-eastwards at
right-angles to the main canal and terminating in a lobe by the
lake shore some 180m south of the present boathouse. This

71. Vertical aerial
photograph taken in
1961, showing Col.
Armstrong's canal
beneath the waters of
Capability Brown's lake.

feature is about the same width as the main canal, and shows on the photograph in a similar fashion, so it may well be a further canal. There is, however, a distinct difference in the junction with the round pond: the entrance of the main canal below the bridge creates a break in the circular edge of the pond, as would be expected, but the rim of the pond is continuous across the exit to the south-east; possibly this represents an additional cascade – a small waterfall is depicted in the foreground of the 1744 painting of the Grand Bridge, though it appears to lie somewhat to the south-east of the position of the round basin. Alternatively, this southern arm may not represent a water feature at all, but some sort of grass terrace or walk. In either case, the canal complex as a whole can be seen to form part of a grand symmetrical design in the same orientation as the palace itself, the state garden and the main avenues.

It is comparatively unusual for submerged features of this nature to shown up so clearly on aerial photographs, and a fortunate combination of circumstances must have occurred on the morning of 15 June 1961, when the photograph was taken, to show the canal so distinctly. The exact time is not recorded, but from the angle of the shadows the sun was fairly low in the sky in an east-by-south direction, which indicates the earlier part of the morning. The lake level seems a little low for the time of year; but although slight traces of the state garden can be discerned in the form of parch-marks south-east of the palace, there is no evidence of extreme drought. Two other critical factors may have conspired to reveal the canal so clearly on this occasion: firstly, the extreme clarity of the water, which is likely to have been a result of earlier dry weather, so that only a small volume of water was being brought into the lake by the Glyme, thereby allowing the silt particles to settle; and secondly, calm conditions with no wind, so that the surface of the water was smooth and reflected no light. Meteorological records from Woodstock and from the nearby Weed Research Organisation at Begbroke show that the rainfall in May 1961 had, indeed, been well below average (0.67 inches, or 15mm, as opposed to the mean of 2.20 inches, or 56mm, for the month), and the dry conditions had continued through the first half of June, with the exception of one heavy shower, which had produced 1.01 inches (26mm) of rain two days before the photograph was taken; the previous dry weather probably resulted in this being rapidly absorbed by the soil, rather than producing a heavy run-off into the lake. The Begbroke records show that the following day, 14 June, was sunny with, significantly, no wind, and the Meteorological Office records show that 15 June itself had started misty, clearing up during the morning, with cumulus developing, the winds being light and mainly southerly, or calm. There had, thus, been a full day for the surface of the lake to settle down before the morning of the photograph, which was itself also generally calm.[6]

Parts of the edges of the main canal, especially the northern side, and to a lesser extent the edges of the round pond, are accentuated by somewhat ragged light markings, which may be weed or algae, or possibly merely the effect of sunlight striking off light surface ripples in the lake. Much of the outline is smooth and uniform, however, and seems to be merely the submerged edges of the canal system revealed through clear, still water. Although no trace of the canal scheme shows on any of the oblique photographs available in the County Museum Service's collections, it does show faintly on two other verticals,

72. The central area of the park in the 1730's.

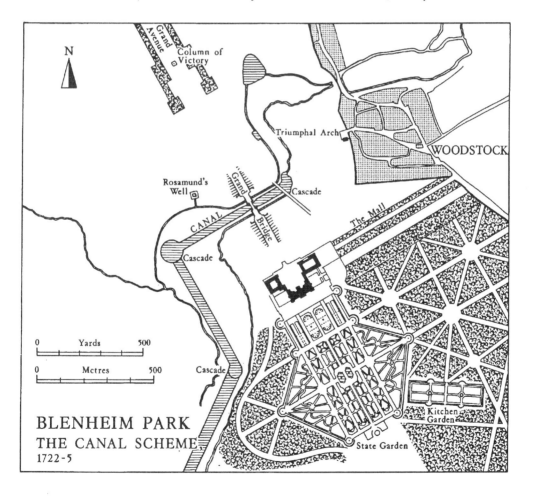

one taken by the R.A.F. in July 1949, and another on a summer afternoon in 1981 by Astral Aerial Surveys for Oxfordshire County Council. This colour print shows the outline of the south-western sector of the pond picked out by an arc of reeds. Elsewhere the canal is wholly submerged but later research has revealed that a third length of canal was actually built.[7]

The canal was in many ways the most interesting and most ambitious of the projects continued by Sarah after Vanbrugh's departure, but work was still continuing elsewhere in the park. The planting of the Grand Avenue out towards the Ditchley Gate included elliptical bays halfway along its length. This would not have been an especially effective feature when viewed from ground level, yet there is no high point from which the pattern of planting could have been appreciated; it certainly lay too far from the palace roof. It is possible that the central ellipse was originally envisaged as the site of a large column incorporating a spiral stairway, rather on the lines of the Monument

73.   The Column of Victory in December 1975, before the felling of the elm avenue.

74. Hawksmoor's Triumphal Arch, the entrance to the park from Woodstock.

75. The Hensington Gate, the entrance to the park from the Oxford road, showing the eastern elm avenue.

in London, from which visitors could look down on the pattern from above. This was never built, however, and we have to give Sarah credit for the present Column of Victory, sited more effectively closer to the palace, right on the skyline of the view from the palace front. Begun in 1727 by the masons Townsend and Peisley, it was a simplified version of a Hawksmoor design, a fluted Doric column 134 feet high, with a lengthy inscription on the base composed by Lord Bolingbroke, and surmounted by a lead statue of the Duke in the guise of a Roman senator, holding aloft a winged Victory and Roman eagles. The statue was by Sir Henry Cheere. The column was completed by Roger Morris for Lord Herbert in 1730.[8]

Sarah also recalled Hawksmoor to complete the Long Library in the Palace and to raise the Triumphal Arch. The arch was at one time attributed to William Chambers, but its design by Hawksmoor has now been established beyond question. It is said that it was originally intended to build the arch on the site of the present Hensington Gate at the entry of the Mall from the Oxford Road, but that this intention was thwarted by the occupation of the critical plot of ground by an obstinate smallholder, who flatly refused to budge: 'No, Sarah,' he is claimed to have said, 'You must go round by the other way.' Whatever the truth of this attractive story, the arch was eventually built in 1723 in a blind corner at the end of the main street of the town of Woodstock; and its impact upon the visitor is magnified tenfold by its very unexpectedness there, and by the glimpse through into the park beyond with Vanbrugh's bridge reflected in Brown's lake. Flanked by Corinthian columns, the arch has a Latin inscription on the town side, with an English translation on the park side.

After Sarah's death in 1744 the park was quiescent for a couple of decades. The vogue for symmetry on the grand scale had run its course, however, and the stage was now set for a new fashion, for the transformation of the park by Lancelot Brown.

Bibliography

CROSSLEY A. 1990: 'Blenheim', in *Victoria History of the County of Oxford*, Vol. XII, pp. 430–70.
GREEN D. 1948: 'Mr Aldersea's Engine', *Manchester Guardian*, 24 Nov. 1948.
GREEN D. 1950: 'Blenheim Column of Victory', *Architectural Review*, April 1950.
GREEN D. 1951: *Blenheim Palace* (Country Life, London), Chs. XV–XIX, pp. 144–182.

References

1   Original plan in Blenheim Estate Office, reproduced in GREEN D. 1951, plate 74, p. 165.
2   Blenheim Muniments F.I.49; this, the Townsend/Peisley contract of 24 April 1722, which includes instructions for the Canals, is quoted in GREEN D. 1951, Appendix XI, p. 313.

3   For Aldersea's engine, see GREEN D. 1948. Aldersea was a drysalter by profession, but an amateur engineer also. At Blenheim he designed a pump, at first sited under the northernmost arch of Vanbrugh's bridge, which raised the water from Rosamund's Well at a rate of 5 tons an hour, up a lift of 120 feet (*c.* 37m) through oaken pipes to the cistern above the kitchen court. According to Stephen Switzer 1715: *The Nobleman, Gentleman and Gardener's Recreation*, this unlikely contraption worked extremely effectively. In the fourth Duke's time the engine was moved to Queen Elizabeth's Island, then to the Pleasure Gardens, and parts of it were finally installed in Woodstock Mill, at the point where the Glyme enters the park, where they remained until comparatively recently.

4   The 1744 painting in Blenheim Palace and the Boydell engravings of 1752 in the Bodleian Library are reproduced in GREEN D. 1951, plates 44, 75 & 87.

5   Fairey Aviation Surveys 6125/8.071–2, 15.6.1961.

6   Meteorological records from the Weed Research Organisation at Begbroke supplied by Mrs C.M. Bond, and from the Meteorological Office at Bracknell by Miss Alison Adam.

7   The R.A.F. photographs, in the form of the Ordnance Survey's 1:10,560 mosaic (ref. SP.41.NW), and the Astral 1981 cover (Photo No. 332) may be consulted in the Oxfordshire Sites and Monuments Record, Centre for Oxfordshire Studies, Oxford. Further information on the waterworks has now been located by Alan Crossley in the Bodleian Library and the Berkshire County Record Office. The east-west length with the round basin was completed by 1723. A shallow lake with a cascade of twelve stone steps was then made above the canal in the following year. In 1724 Townsend and Peisley were contracted to continue the line of the canal southwards from the round basin with three further cascades. Clearly there must have been yet another length of canal, not visible on the 1961 aerial photograph, taking off at an angle of about 45 degrees below the north-south arm, and terminating in an oval basin overflowing back into the old river. See CROSSLEY, A. 1990, pp. 462–3.

8   GREEN D. 1950; see also GREEN D. 1951, pp. 159–60, 170, 173-4, 177, 277-8.

8.   'CAPABILITY' BROWN AT BLENHEIM

Hal Moggridge

76.   Capability Brown's landscape: Blenheim palace in its setting viewed from the east.

IN 1760 A new boy arrived at Eton College. His name was Brown, and almost immediately he acquired the nickname of 'Capey', after his father, Lancelot 'Capability' Brown, who was then, at the age of 44, at the peak of his career. Lancelot Brown the father had enjoyed a meteoric rise to fame as a landscape architect, after leaving school in Northumberland at the age of 16 to become a gardener's boy. From this humble background he had drawn himself up to a position of national pre-eminence by his own energy and genius, on the way acquiring sufficient wealth and status to send his children to Eton. He was, in a sense, a precursor of the great professional engineers of the nineteenth century, and he remained at the summit of his profession until his death on 6 February 1783.

Lancelot Brown's career has been described elsewhere,[1] and need not be pursued in detail here. The main purpose of the present paper is rather to provide a review of his achievement at Blenheim, which amounted to a masterpiece of technical and aesthetic brilliance.

Brown's Achievement at Blenheim

Within a year or two of his son's arrival at Eton, Lancelot Brown was commissioned by the fourth Duke of Marlborough to advise him how to improve the grounds at Blenheim. Before examining Brown's own contribution, it is worth reflecting on the situation which he inherited, and recalling the first Duchess's view quoted earlier by David Green, "tis a chaos, which only God almighty could finish'. Vanbrugh and Wise had left the park adorned with some marvellous individual items – palace, bridge, avenues, tree clumps and parterre – but though each was splendid in its own way, it is difficult to escape the feeling that there was a lack of cohesion between them. For example, etchings made by Boydell in 1752[2] seem to underline the separateness of the items and the bareness of their setting. For all the splendour of the park plan conceived by Wise and Vanbrugh, it remained weak on the ground. For instance, looking up from the bridge, or even from the front of the palace, it was simply not possible to see along the Grand Avenue or to appreciate the grandeur of its lines because of the natural slope of the ground, running away north-westwards beyond the rather steep rise up from the Glyme. Although each feature was magnificent, they failed to fit together in a convincing manner as a large-scale piece of design; it would be of interest to know what someone like Le Nôtre would have managed, given similar circumstances.

Brown's great achievement was to view the huge park of 2,500 acres as a whole, and to transform it into a 'naturalistic' landscape which retained many of the essential features of the earlier design but at the same time brought them together into a single, united composition.[3] The first impact of this upon J.P. Neale in 1823 is worth quoting:

'The scene presented, on entering the Park from this Gate (i.e. the Triumphal Arch), is one of striking grandeur. The House is here seen in an oblique point of view, and its architecture is hence displayed to the greatest advantage; the attention is strongly arrested by the combination of objects that form this most delightful landscape, including, in one view, the Palace, the valley, lake and bridge, amidst plantations of varied tints, and, rising above the trees, the column and statue. . . .[4]

Mavor's description of the same view, published in 1789, is equally graphic:

'On entering the park, one of the most enchanting prospects in nature discloses itself to our view. The Palace appears in front, the towers of which rise into the horizon; on the left, part of the borough of Woodstock; on the right, a broad and deep valley, through which flows a river of equal extent, with bold and winding shores, at a proportionate distance intersected, but visibly not terminated by a Bridge of corresponding magnificence to the grandeur of the scene; a swelling lawn, crowned with a superb and lofty Column, which leaves the tallest trees that seem crowding round its base at an immense distance below, while light clumps, shady groves, and plantations of different shapes and hues skirt the bounding dales, or clothe the remoter slopes; a second reach of water beyond the bridge, fringed by deep woods that rise to the very summit of the opposite hill, and compose a variously tinted and indented surface of luxuriant foliage; all these form an assemblage of attractions unrivalled, and conspire to strike the eye of taste with an irresistible charm. In this singularly picturesque landscape, the beautiful and the sublime are most intimately combined; all that can please, elevate, or astonish, display themselves at once; and the mind is at a loss to know to what source it is chiefly indebted for its pleasure. . . .'.[5]

The central part of the Park, where Brown's design survives largely intact today, still provokes in visitors the same sort of strong emotional reaction. Now, however, instead of merely admiring it in astonishment, we want to know how this wonderful effect was achieved.

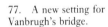

77. A new setting for Vanbrugh's bridge.

The Analysis of Brown's Design

Vanbrugh and Wise had been witty, highly-educated men, who wrote lots of letters and prepared numerous drawings: some 200 letters generated during the course of their work in the park have been deposited in the British Library, and there are at least twenty-three drawings from that period, some design and some working drawings. They provide a very informative, and often very amusing, picture of the relationship between architect and client.

By contrast, Brown's activities at Blenheim appear to be poorly documented. He left only four design drawings of Blenheim, and it has not proved possible to locate significant contemporary correspondence. To assess his contribution, we therefore have to depend on two classes of source material:

(i)   the numerous later drawings, sketches and written descriptions made when Brown's landscape was already maturing;

(ii) observation and measurement of the surviving features made on the ground.

Information from these sources forms the basis for conclusions about Brown's original design, which in turn provides the framework within which restoration proposals can be formulated.

Amongst the written descriptions of the park published shortly after Brown had completed his work there, the most informative is William Mavor's *New Description of Blenheim*, first issued in 1789, and proving so popular with visitors that it had reached its tenth edition by 1817, by which time it contained nearly 150 pages. The frontispiece of Mavor's guidebook is a plan of the park surveyed in 1789 by Thomas Pride, which is not wholly accurate and is a little weak on the detail of the plantations; but it is, nonetheless, of great value in recording the general character of the park at that date, showing the complete layout of the carriage drives, and demonstrating that Brown had retained many of the features of the earlier Wise layout, including the Grand Avenue in the Great Park and all the radiating avenues and circular glades in the Lower Park, in addition to leaving the medieval High Park almost untouched. From this evidence, Brown appears to have conserved virtually everything that his predecessors had left, except for Armstrong's uninspiring canal and the formal garden immediately south of the house. Mavor's text describes the effects which various perambulations and viewpoints produced, and thereby may reveal some of the intentions of Brown's original design; in

78. J.P. Neale's view of the lake, bridge, column and Rosamund's Well, 1823.

particular, the importance of variety in the size and density of plantations and of the views through the open spaces between them is stressed.

The illustrative material available for this period includes thirteen topographical prints and nine watercolours made between 1781 and 1831 now in the Bodleian Library,[6] six engravings made by J.P. Neale in 1823 and now in the Ashmolean Museum, and seven lithographs by C.W. Radclyffe now in the Blenheim Estate Office. These views need to be approached with some wariness. Sometimes later prints were found to be merely copies of earlier ones, made by artists who may never have set foot in Blenheim themselves; these could clearly not be regarded as reliable independent evidence. In other cases distortions had been introduced, especially exaggeration of the vertical scale, to create special graphic effects such as foreshortening. Despite their limitations, however, many of the prints proved to be very accurate in their portrayal of the horizontal arrangement of objects, and provide information available from no other source.

Having analysed the documentary evidence, it then becomes necessary to assess on site the techniques by which the effects were created. The contemporary driveways through the park are the key to this process. Travelling around them at carriage height a series of carefully composed views unfolds one after another. To record this process a series of drawings has been prepared, showing the lines of sight through open space to more distant landmarks from key positions on the perambulation. The alignment of each viewline is critical; in some places it was observed that the ground level of the drive had been slightly raised in order to improve views such as a tantalising glimpse of water between the trees or a long view of lake or palace over a concave-sloping bank. Elsewhere trees were massed to conceal a view of a tower of the palace, which would suddenly be revealed on arriving at the correct viewpoint. It was discovered that the apparently random location of the clumps of trees around the lake was no accident; they occupy the only places where obstruction of the view could be accepted without detracting from the overall effect. Moreover, the very shapes of the clumps were carefully sculpted in order to preserve the series of interlocking sightlines which provide the rich variety of picturesque views over this part of the park. There can be no doubt that Brown's 'naturalistic' design was based upon carefully planned geometric controls every bit as significant and even more complex than those displayed much more obviously by the earlier formal design. The fact that Brown's geometry is not directly perceived has led to a universal underestimate of the precision of his design, so that, in Mavor's words, 'some of his most capital performances have been ascribed to chance.'

Let us now turn to examine the individual elements of Brown's design more closely. These include tree plantations in belts, woods and clumps, open ground, water and buildings.

1. *Ground Modelling*

Boydell's view of 1752 shows that at that date the surroundings of the bridge were still a very stark piece of landscape, the nearest planting being well away from the palace on the north side. The approaches to the bridge were harsh in outline, resembling railway embankments. Brown made something entirely different, reshaping the very form of the ground around the lakes, spoil probably being dug and moved entirely by hand. The result is a soft contour with rounded slopes flanking either side of the new free-form lake and reflecting its sinuous outline.

2. *Water*

The principal water features designed by Brown are: (i) the Great Lakes; (ii) the sinuous River in Lower Park; and (iii) two Cascades supporting each of these two features.

i. *The Lake.* The great lake is the best-known and most striking of the water features, its wonderfully sinuous shape following the curving valley, and also giving purpose to the bridge. In all it occupies an area of some 150 acres. It is a matter of some technical interest how the feat of fixing the level of the

79, 80.   C.W. Radclyffe's *View from Fair Rosamund's Well*, 1842, and the same view in 1983.

lake to suit the bridge was achieved when this was not visible from the top of the dam. Generally contemporary surveys are not impressive in their accuracy. There was, however, a considerable background of water-engineering experience on the Continent, such as Leonardo's work in Milan, that of the brothers Domenico da Viterbo on the Padua Canal in 1481, and the construction of the Antwerp–Brussels canal, begun in 1550 by Jean de Locquenghien. At the time when Brown was working at Blenheim, the first phase of the Canal Age was just beginning in Britain, with Brindley's Bridgewater Canal being completed from Worsley to Manchester in 1761, but not extended through to the Mersey until 1776. Closer to Blenheim was the Stroud-water and Thames & Severn Canal, built between 1759 and 1766, though this was an ill-fated project which never worked very well.[7] Against these faltering steps, Brown's surveying techniques show an extraordinary competence and confidence, and leave no doubt that he was in the forefront of his profession. Holding back this great lake beside the cascade is a quite substantial dam, in which I am assured the original waterworks are still functioning. The sluicegate, though repaired in recent years, still works by its original system. By any standards this represents a quite advanced level of engineering. In order to build a lake of this size today it would be necessary to obtain certification that it was safe from one of twelve nominated specialist dam engineers. Brown was, therefore, faced with and managed to overcome a very difficult technical problem. It is evident from his own preliminary design made in 1765[8] that the

81.   The lower end of the lake, an engraving of c. 1800.

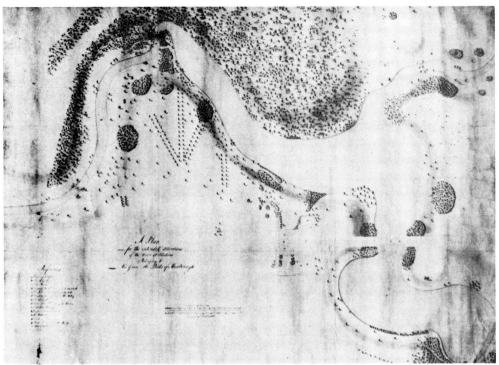

82. Plan for the intended Alterations of the Water at Blenheim, by Capability Brown.

project was modified in detail as work proceeded on site; for example, the preservation of part of the medieval causeway, which crossed the valley to the royal palace, in the form of a long island, was not shown on his original plan.

ii. *The River.* Below the main lake the water is led into a meandering artificial river some 1.5 miles long, running from the foot of the top cascade beneath the bridge in Lower Park, then curving round and getting broader as it continues down the valley, finally curling back towards the Evenlode. In order to make this lowest section into a river rather than another lake, a long side cut and embankment borrowed from canal technology was employed – a quite difficult operation even today, and all the more impressive given that this was made at the very start of the Canal Age.

The River is not so well-known as other parts of Brown's composition today, partly because only the section crossed by the New Bridge is accessible to the public. It made a considerable impression on earlier visitors, however, and Mavor described it thus:

'[Below the Cascade the river] flows with a serpentine sweep through an expanded vale, embellished with scattered groups of flourishing young plantation; ... But though in this reach the river admits an oval woody islet, its channel now becomes more contracted than before; and its style partakes rather of the beautiful than the sublime. Reaching the new bridge, a very elegant structure, it inclines with the course of the vale, and touching near Bladon, makes a determined bend to the right. The banks on both sides at this point are swelling lawn with little clumps connected by single trees, disposed without the least shew of intention. From hence the river takes a variety of charming turns, chiefly with a strong inclination to the right, doubling as it were on itself, and circumscribing the extremity of the hill which accompanies it the greatest part of its course. In one place, a fine sheet of water spreads before the eye, and invites progress by its apparent continuity; in another, the trees seem to embay it, and we advance a considerable way, before we can detect the deception . . . Beyond the river, we are charmed with all the diversity of pleasing scenery: a small grove first presents itself, close to the verge of the tide; a few irregular trees next succeed; sometimes a clump planted at the termination of a reach, by advancing to the belt on the opposite shore, appears to landlock the stream; then again we are delighted with open lawn and diversified landscape. At last, the river precipitates itself down a steep cascade, and at the same instant falls into the Evenlode . . . No awkward termination is here to be traced, no disgusting display of art to heighten the scene; taste unfolds the beauties of Nature with a delicate touch, and Art is only the handmaid to her charms'.[9]

iii. *The Cascades.* 'No awkward termination . . . no disgusting display of art' is the essence of Brown's work here: his art was essentially an invisible one. One particular characteristic was his method of hiding the overflow point. However carefully land-scaped a reservoir or artificial lake may be, one aspect is usually unsatisfactory, namely the view over the top of the dam, which creates a strong horizontal line. At Blenheim the dam is so cleverly placed that one hardly realises it is there. It runs diagonally across the valley, and the cascade lies round the corner, so that from the lake itself one does not actually see the water disappearing over the lip. Similarly at the lower cascade a bridge is carefully placed so as to hide the disappearance of the water from the eye.

Brown's drawing of the upper cascade has survived; its attribution to him is based upon the signature 'L.B., 1764'. It is interesting to see how poor a draughtsman he was; while the scene is recognisable, the drawing fails to pick out any of the elements which make the real cascade such an exciting feature on the ground. On the drawing the top of the cascade is not depicted as being higher than eye-level, and this allows it to show that the rock-work above, still existing on the ground

83. Capability Brown's drawing for the Upper Cascade, 1764.

though now very overgrown, was indeed part of the original intention.[10] As it turned out, however, the cascade as created was far more picturesque and beautiful than the cascade as it was drawn. Clearly it was something other than Brown's actual draughtsmanship which persuaded his clients to spend vast sums of money on putting his schemes into effect.

There is a series of later drawings of the cascade, all made in the nineteenth century. It is of interest that the design work which went into the making of such landscapes effectively preceded their common pictorial depiction. Although they have their ultimate inspiration in Italian paintings of an earlier date, the main series of illustrations begins about fifty years after completion, when the landscapes were beginning to mature and their full effectiveness could be appreciated. Some of the later views show much more effectively than Brown's own drawing the true majesty of the cascade, with its top higher than eye level so that the source of the water remains mysterious and un-known, overhung by trees, and the sheets of water broken up by the rocks. Mavor, too, recorded the cascade when its surroun-dings had grown to maturity:

'Here various trees compose a chequer'd scene,
Glowing in gay diversities of green;
There the full stream thro' intermingling glades,
Shines a broad lake, or falls in loud cascades.

84, 85.   The cascades: lithograph by C.W. Radclyffe, 1842, and photograph by Henry Taunt, *c* 1890.

In the vicinity of the cascade, whose sides are finely shaded, the water is quite lost above. Even from the bridge that fronts it at fifty feet distance, we only see the fall without tracing the supply. The charming reach below appears in its most varied features from this bridge; . . . and when the full stream devolves from the rocky barrier, and bounds from one point to another in foamy pride with deafening roar, nothing can be more grateful to a contemplative mind than such a scene and such a situation'.[11]

3. *Buildings*

Although Brown is best-known as a landscape gardener, he did in fact design a number of buildings, and had an established architectural practice, which was later taken on by his son-in-law, the younger Henry Holland, and later still produced that great architect, John Soane.

The High Lodge, which had already been rebuilt at the beginning of the eighteenth century as a plain, two-storey house with five dormer windows in a steeply-pitched hipped roof, was rebuilt again in the guise of a castellated Gothic folly, with a tall central tower, a semi-hexagonal bay to the east front, and lower flanking wings, all with two-light pointed windows and surmounted with battlements. Although there is no positive proof that this was designed by Brown, it so resembles the general character of his designs that the attribution can hardly

86. High Lodge: lithograph by C.W. Radclyffe, 1842.

87, 88.   High Lodge before and after rebuilding: engraving by John Boydell, 1752, and photograph by Henry Taunt, *c*, 1900.

be in serious doubt.[12] There is an order for wallpaper to be supplied for the lodge in late spring of 1764, which suggests that it had just been completed.[13]

Several other designs for buildings at Blenheim were never built, though drawings for them survive. One of Brown's designs was for the Ditchley Gate, and it is of interest to compare this with Hawksmoor's three alternative designs for the same gate; Brown was careful to set his gate in a landscape context, while Hawksmoor presents it simply as an architectural feature. This again underlines the fundamental difference in the way the park was composed at the two periods, in the earlier period simply a series of magnificent individual elements, in Brown's time envisaged as part of a continuum. Another of Brown's drawings was a design for a Gothic screen with pointed windows, battlements and turrets to conceal the granary, carthorse stables, cart sheds and carter's house at Park Farm. He refers to this in a letter to the Duke dated 26 August 1765, which shows that he was as aware of the practical needs of grain storage as he was concerned that 'the Effect of the Building would be very proper for the situation'.[14] An even more elaborate design, attributed by some to Brown, was for a Gothic bathing-house which was intended to be built at Rosamund's Well, which included a pedimented three-bay façade with ogee-arched two-light windows and quatrefoil lights, its *piano nobile* approached by balustraded segmentally-curved stairways from either flank. The most audacious of all the unfulfilled schemes was a plan for crenellating the park wall and most of the more prominent buildings in the town of Woodstock which were visible from the palace.

89.   The granary at Park Farm: Brown's design of 1765.

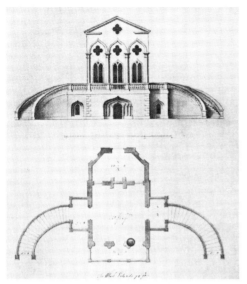

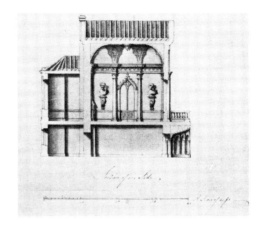

90, 91. Elevations for a proposed Gothic bathing-house at Rosamund's Well.

4. *Planting*

The tree plantations themselves fall into several distinct groups:

i. *Existing plantations retained.* Pride's plan showing the park as it was left by Brown indicates that several elements both of the medieval park and the grand formal layout were retained. Amongst these were the Grand Avenue as planted by Wise, and the walks to the east of the palace. Some large triangular or circular clumps in the northern part of the park had also been planted by Wise, including one very interesting clump with a sort of reverse ha-ha, a wall set below ground surface level in a ditch facing outwards, so that the cattle were unable to get into the wood, though it appears to be standing on open ground.

92. Capability Brown's Plan for the intended alteration from Pritchard's Gate and so on to the new Gates at Oxford Lane, showing the proposed crenellation of the park wall and buildings in the town of Woodstock.

ii. *Shelter-belt.* The Great Park, which must have been a most windswept plateau before Brown came upon the scene, was enclosed with a shelter-belt, which forms a long, low backcloth on the horizon to the nearer clumps, when viewed from within the park. The Great Park is still a huge, bare expanse, exposed to the elements, making up something like half the entire area of the park. It is an important part of the whole composition to have this open space on such a grand scale to contrast with the wooded High Park and sheltered surroundings of the River, which seem all the more intimate, enclosed and private by comparison. Another section of Mavor's view of the park is worth quoting:

> 'The Park . . . is one continued galaxy of charming prospects, and agreably diversified scenes. Its circumference is upwards of twelve miles; its area about two thousand seven hundred acres, round which are the most enchanting rides, chiefly shaded towards the boundary with a deep belt of various trees, evergreens, and deciduous shrubs, whose mingled foliage exhibit the different gradations of tints from the most faint to the most obfuscated green; while plantations of corresponding figure and growth on the park side, sometimes range with the former, and sometimes breaking into groups, with large interstices between, relieve the taedium of continued uniformity, and open the most brilliant prospects'.[15]

Although the composition was primarily in green, there was nonetheless a considerable variety of tone and texture in the choice of trees used.

iii. *The medieval High Park.* Brown appears to have left the High Park largely as it was, a medieval forest of romantic oaks; but it appears that he did cut a few glades in it in order to open up views back to the palace, out towards neighbouring church spires and southwards towards the distant Berkshire Downs. From High Lodge a vista may have been opened up towards Oxford itself. Many of these views have since been lost through later planting.

iv. *Lakeside clumps.* Perhaps Brown's most subtle contribution was the planting of clumps of trees around the edges of the lake as described above, each clump located with great care, and its shape carefully sculpted to admit a whole succession of views.

To appreciate the skill of the planting fully, it is necessary to consider it in relation to the circuit by which visitors were intended to view the park.

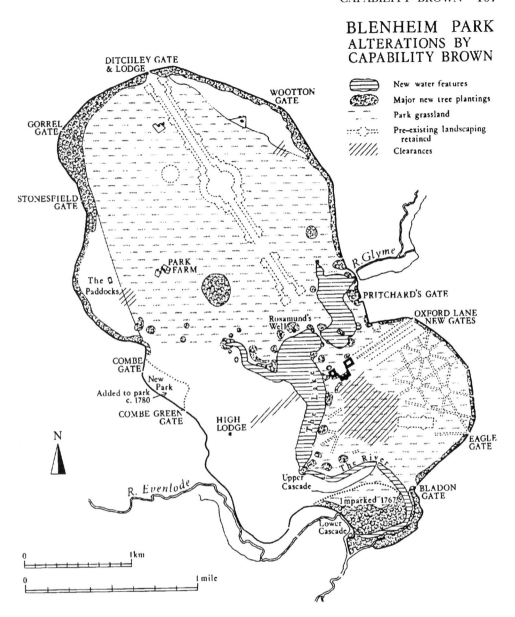

BLENHEIM PARK
ALTERATIONS BY
CAPABILITY BROWN

New water features
Major new tree plantings
Park grassland
Pre-existing landscaping retained
Clearances

DITCHLEY GATE & LODGE
WOOTTON GATE
GORREL GATE
STONESFIELD GATE
R. Glyme
PARK FARM
The Paddocks
PRITCHARD'S GATE
OXFORD LANE NEW GATES
Rosamund's Well
COMBE GATE
New Park
Added to park c. 1780
COMBE GREEN GATE
HIGH LODGE
The Lake
EAGLE GATE
N
The River
Upper Cascade
R. Evenlode
'Imparked' 1767
BLADON GATE
Lower Cascade

0   1 km
0   1 mile

93. Works carried out by Capability Brown at Blenheim.

5. *Drives and walks*

The layout of the carriage drives in the park is shown on Thomas Pride's map of 1789, and described by Mavor thus:

'The drive through the forest wood, which lies between [High Lodge] and the lake, presents such an assemblage of views, and such various combinations of them in rapid succession, that no stranger should omit taking this route. The Water, the Palace, the Gardens, the Grand Bridge, the Pillar, Woodstock, and other near and remote objects, open and shut upon the eye like enchantment; and at one point, every change of a few paces furnishes a new scene, each of which would form a subject worthy of the sublimest pencil'.[16]

It is still possible to walk round this drive today, though some sections of the modern route do not quite follow the original course; and Mavor's description remains equally valid now – every time one visits Blenheim, some new view which one never noticed before comes into sight.

Radclyffe's print of the High Park in 1847[17] shows that it was then more open in appearance, especially along the lakeside. It was probably grazed, which may have had a long-term effect upon its ecosystem, for there has been no regeneration in this area, whereas on the more westerly side, where the slopes face outwards from the park, there has been an interesting regeneration of ancient oaks, the parent tree standing amongst young trees of its own shape and lineage.

94. Thomas Pride's plan of Blenheim Park, 1789.

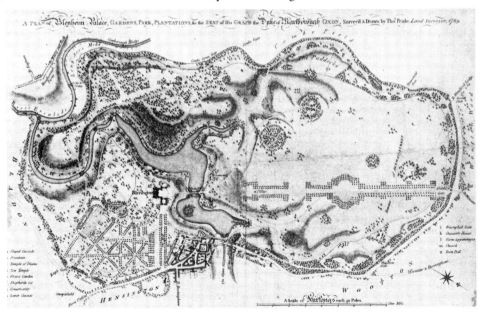

Through High Park and around the lake there was a complicated system of rides giving a series of different visual experiences at different levels. Near the lake one ride followed the shoreline close to water level, and higher up the slope further rides gave views back across or outwards from the park at higher levels. It is worth examining two contrasting short lengths of ride more closely in order to appreciate what Brown was attempting to achieve:

i. *The approach from Woodstock through the Triumphal Arch.* This was the grand approach, giving a series of stunningly impressive views. The first viewpoint came immediately the visitor entered the park through the Triumphal Arch, with the dramatic impact described at the beginning of this chapter. It is, in fact, not the palace as a whole which first catches the eye, but the shape of one of its further towers, the remaining towers being out of sight. The eye then switches to the bridge, and through it, and over it to the distant woodland beyond. The clumps around the lake shore and around the bridge in the middle distance are a critical part of the composition; although the clearings between them look accidental and casual in shape, they do in fact create the lines of vision along which the visitor looks. In one sense this composition resembles a crow's foot of formal spread-out views; but here, instead of laying out the landscape along perspective lines towards vanishing points, Brown has laid out his landscape through informal spaces. Also, instead of moving along those perspective lines, as would have been the case in the traditional classical layout, here the visitor moves transversely to them, towards some new group of vistas from an unexpected spot.

Moving southwards from the Triumphal Arch, the view of the Palace becomes hidden, then the lake slowly becomes obscured by a dense clump of trees on the right, now sadly thinned out and reduced by age, though recently replanted. The view of the palace reappears, with its towers framed boldly by the trees – only these are not the same towers visible from the Arch. Identical towers contribute to this part of the composition; the sense of space and distance travelled is subtly increased by the fact that the first view seen is of the most far-off tower, which disappears, and then when the palace reappears it is the closer tower which is seen, seeming unexpectedly near; the mind, adapted to judging distance by size, registers the whole scheme as being on an even grander scale than, in reality, it is.

The driveway turns right into one of Wise's retained avenues. Shortly before the Palace is reached, there is another angled glimpse of the bridge with a composition of very distant views

95, 96.   Views of the lake photographed by Henry Taunt, *c.* 1890.

away to the right, extending to the furthest boundaries of the park.

When all the significant views in every direction are studied, the intersecting mesh of view-lines between the clumps to more distant features is of staggering complexity. We do not know how this precision was achieved. It clearly was not done by drawing. My own view of Brown's method, albeit entirely hypothetical, is that he had a very brilliant conception of ground in three dimensions; and that, when coming on a site visit, he would carry in his mind all the while a three-dimensional vision of views which he had already decided upon; in this way he was able to set out an extremely complex system of views by site instructions without ever laying pen to paper or intercepting a view previously designed with plantations to frame a new view.

Four groups of trees between the southern abutment of the bridge and the palace front are an especially good example of this principle. Each clump is different in shape and size, so that they form an interesting series of features in the landscape in their own right. The controlling lines of space between the clumps are carefully related to the network of views. The clumps on either side of the bridge are wedge-shaped, so that from the mid-point of the bridge the entire width of the palace façade can be appreciated, rather than merely the centre, as would have been the case with a straight avenue at this point. The four clumps are sculpted to admit a whole series of views over different aspects of the lake or back towards the palace. Closer to the palace there was even a single tree, carefully sited in the only possible position in which a single tree would not block key views from one place or another. Similarly every single clump in the key area in the centre of the park is exactly shaped to create the great composition.

ii.   *The carriage drive*. The clockwise journey around the long southern carriage drive is of an altogether different character, at first providing only a series of glimpses and hints of what is to come, before ending up on the bridge with a really grand view. Through the oakwoods of High Park, there are occasional momentary distant views of a tower on the palace, or of the water below. Further along, glimpses of the Column begin to appear; then a distant view of the Seven Arches Bridge at the head of the lake, which used to have Lombardy Poplars on either side.[18] Until this point the drive has provided a series of interesting glimpses at widely-spaced intervals, to be taken in on a slow, meandering progress; but as the bridge is approached the tempo of the changes quickens and the impact of the views is considerably increased, with ever more dramatic vistas

97.   Aerial view of the drive from the Triumphal Arch to the palace, overlaid with key viewlines.

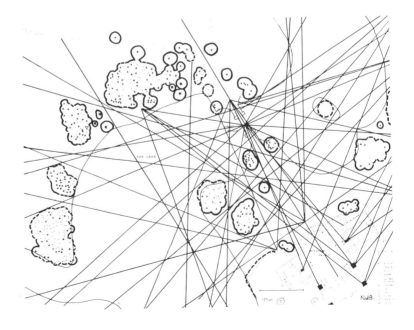

98.   Plan of viewlines overlaid on survey of eighteenth-century trees surviving in 1983.

succeeding each other at closer intervals. Finally, the views from the centre of the bridge itself mark the climax of the journey. In front the entire width of the façade of the palace is seen between the two clumps of trees, cut back as described above, displaying Vanbrugh's grand design at its very best. In other directions, wherever one looks, there are distant or close views of immense grandeur. The different textures of the cedars and beeches are beautifully composed together. One of the characteristics of this type of design is the different values one gets as the light changes, so typical of England: at one time it is the distant woods or the water which are highlit, at other times one or another face of the building.

The character of these two short journeys through parts of Brown's landscape is quite different, the composition intended to affect the emotions in entirely different ways. The first is as grand a series of vistas as could be achieved, intended to impress and astonish the new visitor, holding the tension high until the palace itself is reached. The second is mainly low-key, a more gradual and contemplative circuit for the day-to-day use of the family and resident visitors, which only gradually builds up to a single major dramatic effect at the bridge as the journey ends.

Brown's clumps of trees were so carefully judged that, even in their full maturity, long after his death, the views he had composed were maintained. Today, however, his plantings are coming to the end of their life. The great beech plantations are dying of old age, a situation exacerbated by the dry summers of 1976 and 1981, and this is why the eleventh Duke has commissioned a restoration plan. It is an interesting reflection of changing attitudes and the way in which each generation thinks of its surroundings and responds to what is popular in its own age, that the present Duke should undertake a restoration, whereas his forebears with equal enthusiasm commissioned great plans for sweeping away large parts of what they had inherited and redesigning in new styles. In an age which values history so much, it is appropriate that an exact reconstruction of Brown's landscape should be pursued.

Bibliography

CLIFFORD J. 1974: *Capability Brown: an Illustrated Life of Lancelot Brown, 1716–1783* (Shire Lifelines series No.33, Shire Publications, Princes Risborough).
GREEN D. 1951: *Blenheim Palace* (Country Life).
HYAMS E. 1971: *Capability Brown and Humphry Repton* (J.M. Dent & Sons, London).
MAVOR W. 1789: *New Description of Blenheim* (1st edn.).
MOGGRIDGE H. 1984: The Working Method by which the Original Composition of Planting around L. Brown's Lakes was Defined, *Landscape Research* Vol. 9 No. 2, pp. 15–23.

NEALE J.P. 1823: *An Historical Description of Blenheim, with Six Views.*
STROUD D. 1950: *Capability Brown* (new edn., Faber & Faber, London, 1975).

References and Footnotes

1   STROUD D. 1950; HYAMS E. 1971; CLIFFORD J. 1974.
2   E.g. Bodl. Gough Maps 26, Nos. 55 & 56; G.A. Oxon.a.79, p. 45, Nos. 33–37.
3   MOGGRIDGE H. 1984.
4   NEALE J.P. 1823, p. 4.
5   MAVOR W. 1st edn. 1789, p. 37; this view is the subject of a lithograph of 1842 by C.W. Radclyffe (Blenheim Estate Office).
6   Bodl. G.A. Oxon.a.79, Nos. 41–46 (prints of views of lake); Bodl. MS. Top. Oxon. a.69, Nos. 624–9 (six monochrome watercolours by J. Buckler, 1827–1830); Bodl. Gough Maps 26, Nos. 50, 56 (two watercolours of 1781); Bodl. Dep.d.145, frontispiece (watercolour of view from Woodstock Rectory by J.C. Buckler, 1823). Ashmolean XXX VIIA (J.P. Neale engravings).
7   *Cf.* SINGER C., HOLMYARD E.J., HALL A.R. & WILLIAMS T.I. (Eds.) 1957: *A History of Technology*, Vol. III (Clarendon Press, Oxford), pp. 438–470, q.v. for further references to the continental background. See also GLADWIN D.D. & WHITE J.M. 1968: *English Canals*, Vol. II: *Engineers and Engineering* (Oakwood Press, Lingfield); HANDFORD M. 1979: *The Stroudwater Canal* (Alan Sutton, Gloucester); and HOUSEHOLD H. 1983: *The Thames & Severn Canal* (new edn., Alan Sutton, Gloucester).
8   'A Plan for the Intended Alterations of the Water of Blenheim, belonging to His Grace the Duke of Marlborough,' by L. Brown, 1765 (Blenheim Estate Office).
9   MAVOR W.: 1st edn. 1789, pp. 121–4.
10 Sketch of 1764 by L. Brown (Blenheim Estate Office).
11 MAVOR W.: 1st edn. 1789, p. 98.
12 STROUD D. 1975 edn., Plate 29b, pp. 130–1.
13 GREEN D. 1951, p. 231.
14 Blenheim Muniments, letter quoted by STROUD D. 1975 edn., p. 131.
15 MAVOR W. 1st edn. 1789, p. 126.
16 MAVOR W. 10th edn. 1817, p. 97.
17 Lithographs of views in the grounds by C.W. Radclyffe, 1842 (Blenheim Estate Office, box).
18 *Cf.* THOMPSON J. 'Remarks on the Effect of the Lombardy Poplar in Park Scenery', *The Gardener's Magazine* Vol. 1, 1826, p. 17.

99. George, fourth Duke of Marlborough with his eldest son, painted by Sir Joshua Reynolds, 1778.

9. AFTER CAPABILITY BROWN: BLENHEIM IN THE LATER EIGHTEENTH AND EARLY NINETEENTH CENTURIES

David Green, James Bond & Hal Moggridge

William Chambers and the Gardens in the Home Park

David Green & James Bond

WHILE Lancelot Brown was working in the park, the embellishment of the palace had been put into the capable hands of William Chambers. Even before Brown's departure in 1774, Chambers had put forward suggestions for new buildings and ornamental features in the grounds, and the fourth Duke sanctioned changes to the first Duchess's flower-garden outside the east front of the palace, and a whole series of additions to the landscape in the Lower Park and its surroundings during the 1770s and 1780s.

The New Bridge

One of Chambers's designs was for the New Bridge on the Bladon side of the park, half a mile below the cascade. A graceful balustraded structure of three arches, this was completed on the site of an earlier bridge in 1773.

Temples in the Pleasure Grounds

Chambers was also involved in the design of at least one of the little temples which were dotted about in the Pleasure Grounds during this period.[1] The Temple of Diana, on a high point commanding a splendid view over the lake to the woods beyond, has a pediment bearing a dedication to Diana, supported by four pillars with Ionic capitals. Inside, on the rear wall, is a medallion with a representation in bas-relief of Hippolytus offering a wreath to Diana, together with some appropriate verses from Euripides. Another of the garden buildings, the Temple of Health, was designed by John Yenn, architect of the new tower of Woodstock church, to commemorate the recovery of King George III from illness; built in 1789, it is open-fronted, with a pediment supported on either side by a pair of Corinthian columns, the rear wall bearing a bas-relief medallion portrait of the king incorporated into a painted scene of a column, steps and balustrade. The fifth Duke subsequently

100.   The New Bridge and Bladon Church from the gardens: lithograph by C.W. Radclyffe, 1842.

101.   The New Bridge from the Bladon side today.

Temples in the Pleasure Grounds:
102. Temple of Diana
103. Temple of Health
104. Temple of Flora

attached an aviary to Yenn's temple, and began a garden in front of it. A third temple, the Temple of Flora, is the least ambitious architecturally, consisting merely of an open-fronted alcove framed in an elliptical keystoned arch, with the pediment above enclosing an empty wreath. Its modest form was, however, enhanced by the beauty of its setting: according to Mavor,[2] 'during the summer months, every interstice left by the trunks of the surrounding grove is replenished with oranges, lemons, and other exotic trees, shrubs and plants of the greatest delicacy and the richest odour . . .' The temples at Blenheim hark back to the designs of William Kent at Rousham in the 1730s, and their appearance here is almost anachronistic; generally the fashion for mock Greek temples was in decline by the third quarter of the eighteenth century.[3]

The Gardens around the Cascade

The most elaborate alterations took place in the area below the Cascade, initiated by the fourth Duke and continued by his successor. The Springlock Lodge takes its name from a trick feature which had been installed on the path on the steep bank above the waterfall. Here the visitor, delicately picking his way along the edge of the miniature precipice intended by the Duke to conjure up the sort of wild and rugged scenery depicted by the seventeenth-century Italian painter Salvator Rosa, was led round a corner only to find his route blocked by a huge, unhewn boulder.[4] However, a slight touch of the hand allowed the rock to swing back by a hidden spring, to allow access through to 'a spot in the highest style of picturesque beauty', where the Duke

105. The Bernini fountain in its original position below the Cascade: photograph by Henry Taunt, 1909.

had set up the great fountain which had been presented to the first Duke in 1710 by the Spanish ambassador to the Papal Court: a splendid affair in the style of Bernini, with four river-gods representing the great rivers of the four continents, Danube, Nile, Plate and Ganges, disporting themselves around a rugged, caverned rock which is surmounted by a white marble obelisk. A lion and a seahorse guard the entrance to the cavern, and the arms of Leon and Castile appear on one side on the base of the obelisk. The fountain had been somewhat damaged during its long period of storage, and was reassembled somewhat clumsily below the Cascade; it has since been removed from here to a new site on the water terraces near the Palace.[5]

The fifth Duke, succeeding to the title in 1817, embarked upon a plan to create around the Cascade 'the finest botanical and flower garden in England',[6] taking full advantage of the availability of the exotic species which were then being brought into Britain by plant collectors in all corners of the globe. Down below the waterfall and alongside the River he laid out the Botany Bay Garden, the Chinese Garden and the Dahlia Garden, 'all surrounded with borders of seedling oaks, kept constantly cut'. Further buildings and other structures appeared amongst the plantings. Higher up the bank, a timbered Swiss cottage was built to accommodate the watchman to the private gardens, with roundel windows and a curious spired turret at the gable end.[7] On the island below the Cascade a rustic Shepherd's Cot was built. A mock Cromlech or Druid's Temple was also erected. Apart from the great cedars, swamp cypresses and a few other exotic features, however, little of these gardens has survived.

106.   Rock gardens below the Cascade: engraving by W.A. Delamotte, *c.* 1820.

107. The Rock Gardens: photograph by Henry Taunt, *c.* 1900

108. The River Glyme below the Cascade: photograph by Henry Taunt, *c.* 1890.

109. The rustic bridge and summerhouse in the Pleasure Grounds: photograph by Henry Taunt, *c.* 1890.

110   The Springlock
Lodge today.

Blenheim: The Legacy of Capability Brown

Hal Moggridge

On 13 August 1787 Blenheim was visited by the Hon. John Byng, later the fifth Viscount Torrington. He recorded his impressions, which are of particular interest as a description of the park shortly after Lancelot Brown's death, when the tide of public opinion was turning against Brown's work and when many aspects of the design were still immature or partly-complete:[8]

'... I betook myself to the pleasures of Blenheim Park; and therein did I sit, walk, moralize, and criticize for 3 hours: Blenheim Park is a great and fine thing; that we all acknowledge; but the Duke is sparing of plantations, and it is evident that his great planner Brown is dead: all the sides of the lake shou'd be planted, as well as numbers of acres, and thousands of single trees, and thorns, in the grand front. The Duke sticks up 12 trees here, and 13 there, but that is poor work! And why all beeches? Variety is the life of planting. To suppose a place at first nobly grand – as nature gave it – it shou'd be all wood and water; and then taste shou'd cautiously scoop out the glades and thin the lawns: therefore no man can plant too much; let him cover his ground with trees, and he will then best see where to open views.

I wander'd over the spot, whereon stood the royal manor house; by Rosamund's Well; by the river side, for an hour; and then return'd by the column, with Queen Anne at the top; (aye, thought I, thou art an ugly pile, and had better be pull'd down, with most of the elm trees around thee) and by overtopping the trees makes them appear dwarfish: here I read, for some time,

about Ramilles, Malplaquet, and our other ruinous glories . . .
The worst thing abt. Blenheim is the vicinity of the town, whence
come eternally all the horrid noises of dogs, bells, &c &c – surely
the Duke of M. shou'd along the wall of the town leading from
the entrance, plant copiously, and not permit the full gape of all
those houses upon his park; and, even, they wou'd be benefited
by the obstruct of the western sun; and still might catch every
view, when allow'd, from branches or trees fell'd. The new
steeple of Woodstock Church adds a beauty to the park; but why
not a Gothic, instead of a Grecian temple? Sr. J. Vanbrugh's
shade still presides in this neighbourhood'.

Woodstock church tower had just been rebuilt in 1785 to the
design of John Yenn, as a square, four-stage tower with
rusticated quoins, a balustraded parapet with four-stage corner
pinnacles, bell-openings in large round-arched recesses, and
swags in panels below the parapet with larger swags on either
side of the clock-face. This had been selected in preference to
the more graceful but more costly design prepared by William
Chambers in 1776, which would have had three principal stages,
the lower two rusticated, with urn finials at the corners, carrying
a fourth octagonal balustraded stage with more urn finials,
carrying in turn a slender obelisk with yet another urn on the top.[9]
The following morning Byng visited the gardens closer to the
palace in a less choleric frame of mind: 'If I, before, bore hard
upon some points of the D. of M.'s taste, and have heard others
accuse him of parsimony, we must recant when we enter upon
these walks, and shall see the pleasure grounds in such
perfection; and shall learn that 50 people are daily employ'd in
his gardens, and 100 more in the park &c: they will then exclaim
with me "These are imperial works and worthy (of) Kings"; and
that the post office grant is very unequal to the expenditure . . .'
He went down to the cascade, 'within the sweet spot lately
enclosed by the duke, and only disfigured by a pitiful, Frenchly-
adorn'd fountain, close to the gt. water; which fountain wou'd
have appear'd in pretty propriety in the flower garden: the
Chinese bridge is also of mean effect.' He then went across the
park to the Menagerie, where the Duke had followed the
precedent of his royal predecessor, Henry I, by establishing an
enclosure for exotic beasts. 'In the menagerie (a dirty, shabby
place) are kept two beautiful deer call'd blue cow deer, from the
East Indies; a remarkably fine Spanish ass, (from whom all the
fine mules who work in the park are descended;) and two moose
deer from America, the oddest shapen, and ugliest animals I
ever saw, with heads of asses, bodies of every ill shape, and with
legs so thin and long, that they appear like spiders of fifteen

hands high'. Another occupant of the menagerie, not mentioned by Byng, was a tiger sent by Lord Clive to the Duke of Marlborough in 1771.[10] Elsewhere, 'In various parts of the park are clusters of faggots around a coop, where are hatch'd and rear'd such quantities of pheasants that I almost trod upon them in the grass'.

Another visitor, a few years later in April 1786, was Thomas Jefferson, who took in Blenheim during the course of a short tour of the most notable English parks and gardens. Despite his generally lukewarm attitude to much of what he saw, he was undoubtedly impressed with Blenheim. Like Byng, he drew particular attention to the labour-force needed to maintain the park and gardens:

> '2500 as., of which 200 is garden, 150 water, 12 kitchen garden and the rest park. 200 people employed to keep it in order, and to make alterations and additions. About 50 of these employed in pleasure grounds. The turf is mowed once in 10 days in summer. About 2000 fallow deer in the park, and 2- or 3000 sheep . . . Rosamund's bower was near where there is now a little grove about 200 yards from the palace. The water here is very beautiful and very grand'.[11]

Between Lancelot Brown's retirement from Blenheim in 1774 and the present day, the landscape which he created underwent a number of modifications.

One of the most obvious changes has simply been the effect of old age, as after two centuries of working well, his plantations have come to the end of their natural life. Nothing whatever can be done about this, other than to start again and wait for fifty or a hundred years until the same effect reappears. Indeed, the restoration plan which will be explained in Chapter 11 has turned out to be on a two-hundred-year cycle.

The first edition of Mavor's guide included Pride's survey. From about the seventh edition (c.1810) a revised plan was included, which showed two significant changes:

i.   The main avenue to the Ditchley Gate has been broken up into discontinuous fragments: this represents a sort of deformalisation process, an attempt to mould into the 'Capability' Brown style every feature which was not Brown's originally.

ii.   Big agricultural enclosures were taking place in the Great Park, in line with changing thoughts on what was important in the landscape. This seems of no harm aesthetically, as the agricultural landscape is as fine as the great expanse of bare grassland would have been.

The first Ordnance Survey 1:2500 map of the 1880s shows that many of the earlier formal features which Brown had conserved had, by now, been removed; he has often been wrongly blamed for this. The reason for their removal was probably that, as Brown's landscape developed into its full maturity, the feeling arose that nothing should be allowed to remain which was not part of his own design. However, this was a slight misunderstanding of Brown's original vision, which had been to bring together elements from different ages into a great united overall design.

The landscaping works carried out by the ninth Duke between 1890 and 1935 would clearly warrant a major study in their own right. It is remarkable that, at the time when great amateurs were creating their own landscapes in the eighteenth century, the fourth Duke had employed a professional, while in the late nineteenth century, when many other estate-owners were tinkering around with petty little works, the ninth Duke of

111. The Lake and Pleasure Grounds: late eighteenth- and nineteenth-century features

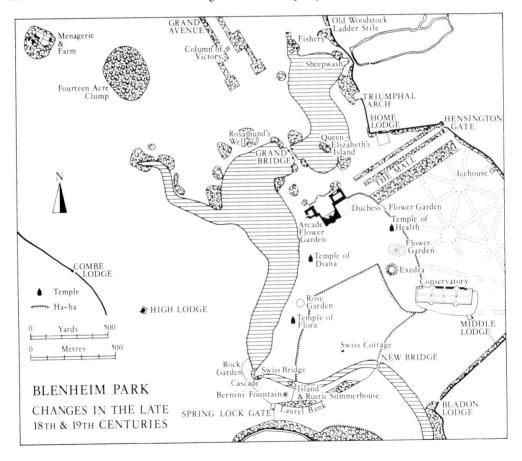

Marlborough saw Blenheim as a whole and undertook a huge scheme of refurbishment. Had he not embarked upon this work, given that Brown's planting is now reaching the end of its life, we could envisage being left with almost nothing in a few decades' time. The ninth Duke carried out several major works:

i.   The creation of new formal gardens near the palace, made by Achille Duchêne, which will be discussed further by David Green in Chapter 10.

ii.   The replanting of the Grand Avenue to a layout different from and even grander than the original, but in the same position. This will also be described further by David Green in the following chapter.

iii.   The restoration of the avenues to the east of the palace.

iv.   The introduction of a number of new clump plantings in the valleys, alternating with Brown's clumps. For these, trees with coloured foliage have frequently been introduced in response to the ninth Duke's view that 'the combination of the two colours, the copper and the grey, ought to be most effective and picturesque'.[12]

Some of the ninth Duke's plantations around the lake were unfortunate, in that they blocked out some of the views which Brown had so carefully contrived; obviously one task for the future is to consider whether it would be sensible to fell these trees and to reopen these views. However, elsewhere his clumps have provided the necessary continuum, even if, in the short term, they have created a more densely-wooded scene than Brown envisaged; when Brown's own trees have to be removed as they reach the end of their life in the next few decades, the ninth Duke's trees will remain, until the modern replanting of Brown's layout has itself matured.

112.   The Swiss Cottage at Blenheim.

In spite of all the natural hazards of storm, fire and drought, and in spite of later alterations to the park, it is remarkable how much of Lancelot Brown's great work of art has come down to us. In Mavor's words, 'Glades, lawns, gentle hills, retiring vales, wood and water, so sweetly blend and harmonise in the landscape, that the eye every where finds novelty and interest, and acknowledges the effect of contrast and design, without revolting at its display . . . Here a thousand beauties, originating from design, appear fortuitous to the eye.'[13] So what of the future? This park has become a place where hundreds of thousands of people find emotional refreshment. Will that be so two hundred years from now? The present Duke has inherited the great task of preservation, and the problems of present and future management will be explored in Chapter 11.

References

1   SHERWOOD J. & PEVSNER N. 1974: *The Buildings of England: Oxfordshire* (Penguin, Harmondsworth), p. 474.

2   MAVOR W.F. 1811: *New Description of Blenheim* (8th edn.), p. 62.

3   *Cf.* WOODWARD F. 1982: *Oxfordshire Parks* (Oxfordshire Museum Services Publication No.16), Chs. 3 & 4; it is here suggested that the more intricate and inward-looking development of the pleasure-grounds south of Blenheim Palace, with its revived interest in ornamental plantings and small follies, represents the beginnings of the reaction against Brown's wide open spaces and sweeping panoramic views.

4   MAVOR W. F. 1835: *New Description of Blenheim* (12th edn.), pp. 58–9; W.A. Delamotte's drawing of the Springlock Boulder is reproduced in the guidebook by GREEN D. 1972: *Blenheim Park & Gardens* (Blenheim Estate Office), p. 29.

5   GREEN D. 1951: 'The Bernini Fountain at Blenheim', *Country Life* Vol. CX, 268.

6   MAVOR W.F. 1835: *New Description of Blenheim* (12th edn.), p. 58.

7   An engraving of the Swiss cottage is reproduced in GREEN D. 1951: *Blenheim Palace* (Country Life), p. 191.

8   BRUYN ANDREWS C. (Ed.) 1934: *The Torrington Diaries, containing the Tours through England and Wales of the Hon. John Byng, between the years 1781 and 1794* (Eyre & Spottiswoode, London), Vol. 1, pp. 322–329.

9   COLVIN H.M. 1949: 'The Rebuilding of Woodstock Church Tower (1770–1786)', *Oxfordshire Archaeological Society Report* No. 87, pp. 9–14.

10 GRETTON M.S. 1902: *Three Centuries in North Oxfordshire*, quoting *Jackson's Oxford Jnl.*

11 JEFFERSON T. 1786: *Memoranda of a Tour of the Gardens of England*, in *Picturesque Taste and the Garden*, p. 336; see also BETTS E.M. 1944: *Thomas Jefferson's Garden Book, 1766–1824.*

12 THE NINTH DUKE OF MARLBOROUGH: *Trees planted at Blenheim* (The red planting record book, Blenheim Estate Office), p. 14.

13 MAVOR W. 1817: *New Description of Blenheim* (10th edn.), p. 94; ibid. (1789, 1st edn.), p. 114.

10. BLENHEIM: THE CONTRIBUTION OF ACHILLE DUCHÊNE AND THE NINTH DUKE

David Green

WHEN THE eighth Duke died in 1892, his heir immediately cabled from America: 'Dredge lake'; and on his return he lost no time in restoring the three-acre forecourt on the north to its original form. This marked the start of an energetic campaign of restoration in the park.

The original Grand Avenue was by now in a poor condition, and nineteenth-century maps show that it had been reduced to a series of discontinuous blocks. In 1896 the ninth Duke wrote: 'I have replanted the north avenue (with elms), believing that in the year 2000 it will form a remarkable feature in the Park, extending as it does for nearly two miles'. This replanting was completed in 1902, on a slightly different pattern to the original, with a lozenge feature creating an illusion of branching avenues in place of the original central ellipse. The Duke added a caution, however: 'Any man who cuts these trees down for the purpose of selling the timber is a scoundrel, and deserves the worst fate that can befall him'. Dying in 1934, he was never to know that the scoundrel which would cause the downfall of his avenue within the space of fifty years was no man, but a beetle: Dutch elm disease.

'The planting of oaks in the High Park', he added in 1898, 'should be continued for another 25 years, and then the Park will be stocked for 500 years to come'. Between 1893 and 1919 he enriched his estate with no fewer than 465,000 trees. Certainly it was no fault of his, nor of his successors, that, in Hardy's phrase, 'God sent a worm to madden his handywork' (or perhaps it was the Devil who sent the beetle). It is good to record, however, that the present Duke has begun to recoup the damage once more: the great north avenue has been replanted with two kinds of lime, while for the eastern approach he has restocked the Mall from the Hensington Gate with alternating planes and limes, the first of the limes there having been planted by the Prince of Wales on 19 December 1976.

The lawns which Lancelot Brown had created, sweeping up to the palace, had become partly overgrown with gloomy Victorian shrubberies, and the ninth Duke decided to clear these and replace them with new formal gardens to give the palace a more fitting setting and recall something of the style of the long-vanished Great Parterre. To effect this transformation he called in the French landscape-architect Achille Duchêne.

Duchêne began on the site of Sarah's eastern parterre

113. Charles, ninth Duke of Marlborough with his younger son, Lord Ivor, on his knee. His heir, Lord Blandford, stands on the Duke's right. August 1910.

114.   The Water Terraces: Achille Duchêne's design.

between the east wing and the orangery, laying out a formal
garden in Italian style, with tubbed orange-trees, statues and
swirling arabesques of dwarf box. Its centrepiece was a round
pool with a gilded Venus holding aloft a ducal coronet through
which a fountain sprays. This was the work of the American
sculptor Waldo Story, whom the Duke and his first American
Duchess, Consuelo Vanderbilt, had befriended in Rome; it was
completed and installed in c.1910.

115.   The east front and
formal garden before the
fountain: photograph by
Henry Taunt, c. 1900.

116.   Waldo Story's
fountain in the Italian
Garden.

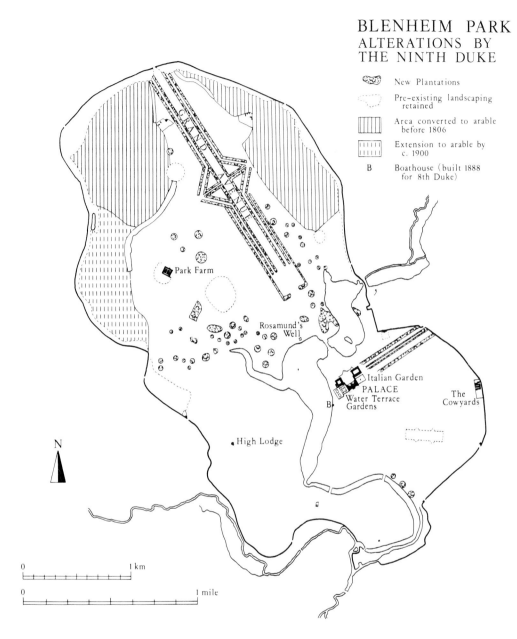

BLENHEIM PARK
ALTERATIONS BY
THE NINTH DUKE

New Plantations

Pre-existing landscaping
    retained

Area converted to arable
    before 1806

Extension to arable by
    c. 1900

B   Boathouse (built 1888
    for 8th Duke)

GRAND AVENUE

Park Farm

Rosamund's
Well

Italian Garden

PALACE
Water Terrace
Gardens

B

The
Cowyards

High Lodge

N

0   1 km

0   1 mile

117. Works initiated by the ninth Duke.

Last of all, having ensured formal settings for the palace on
north and east (the south was too vast even for him to restore),
the ninth Duke devoted five of his last years, from 1925 to 1930,
to transforming a dull shrubbery on the west into two French-

118.   The west front
and lawn before the
Water Terraces:
photograph by Henry
Taunt, *c.* 1890.

style water-terraces, to make together a princely *parterre d'eau* on
the model of Versailles, a work worthy of Vanbrugh, if not
precisely in his manner. One of several strange phenomena
which the Duke insisted upon was the feeding of the fountain-
basins with water from Rosamond's Well which, he believed,
had some mystical quality, even though this meant piping that
magic water the length of the western lake before pumping it
back uphill to his water terraces. From the start Duchêne was
directed to work less in the spirit of Le Nôtre than in that of
Bernini, whose *modello* for his river-gods fountain in the Piazza
Navona in Rome was to have the place of honour on the second
terrace. When, later, Duchêne pleaded for more fountains, he
was firmly told: 'Limpidity of water posseses a romance. You
have got this effect in the basins and in the large area of water
contained by the Lake. Be careful not to destroy this major
emotion which Nature has granted you, for the sake of what may
possibly be a vulgar display of waterworks which can be seen at
any exhibition or public park'. Despite this, Duchêne went
ahead with his fountains in defiance of the Duke's wishes; and
when at last, in 1930, the terraces were finished, the Duke was
magnanimous enough to congratulate his garden architect and
to acknowledge his genius in an inscription to be seen on the
south wall of the chapel.

And so, from remote beginnings out to the undiscovered
ends, there surely run two strong threads creating and binding
all together: water, from the never-failing spring of Rosamond's
Well and from the modest Glyme; and thought, creative

119, 120.   The Water Gardens today: the upper terrace and the row of caryatids below.

thought, from successive owners of Blenheim and from their architects. 'Turn all these matters over in your mind', wrote the ninth Duke to Duchêne, 'when you are at rest in the evening; for it is only by thought, constant thought and mature reflection, that artists have left their great works for the enjoyment of posterity'.

References

GREEN D. 1951: *Blenheim Palace* (Country Life, London), Ch. XXII, pp. 203–218.
GREIG B.J.W. 1981: 'The History of the Elm Avenues at Blenheim and Dutch Elm Disease', *Jnl of Forestry* Oct. 1981, pp. 207–213.

11. BLENHEIM: PRESENT MANAGEMENT AND FUTURE RESTORATION

Ralph Cobham & Paul Hutton

Problems of Present Maintenance

Paul Hutton

TWO OF THE problems of maintenance mentioned in earlier papers are every bit as relevant today. Firstly, the reference in the thirteenth century to the work involved in maintaining the park wall strikes a very familiar chord: we spend a very considerable number of man-hours maintaining and repairing the park wall today. The second point, following Hal Moggridge's comment about the lake dam, is that in order to comply with the legislation under the Reservoirs Safety Provision Act of 1930, we are required to have the dam inspected regularly by one of the panel of civil engineers charged with this responsibility. In 1982 we spent £18,000 on the maintenance of the dam alone, in order to stop it leaking. Now, having done some work to the lake dam immediately adjoining the cascade, we are having to look at the rather longer dam which holds the Bladon lake, and it will be necessary to carry out further works there this year, again to prevent leakage. So, the level of expenditure on maintaining the park is high.

When the eleventh Duke succeeded to the estate, he inherited two particular problems. Firstly, the attack of Dutch Elm Disease had disastrous effects. The avenue from the Palace to the Hensington Gate was felled and replanted in 1976, as David Green has recorded, with Prince Charles planting the first tree. Immediately after completion of that avenue, a beginning was made on the Grand Avenue to the north-west. This was felled and replanted over a period of three years. One of the major problems of dealing with such a vast amount of timber was that it was necessary virtually to establish a mobile sawmill, operating in three places within the park while the timber was being felled. The best lengths went to the furniture industry, the second-quality lengths went for mining timber, and the remainder went for firewood. It was a very sad and depressing thing for all of us involved in the management of the park, as the sawmill moved remorselessly up the avenue.

Along the line of the avenue one single beech tree survived, and it was decided that it would be wrong to fell a healthy living tree, although it may cause something of a problem in fifty years time when it has to come out in its turn, leaving a gap in the

121.   H.R.H. the Prince of Wales, accompanied
by the present Duke of Marlborough, plants the
first lime tree in the restored eastern avenue,
19 December 1976.

avenue. The present replanting of the Grand Avenue was carried out over a three-year period, beginning in the winter of 1977, with a second stage in 1978 and the final stage in 1979. Two rows of lime on either side of the drive were planted, at a total cost of approximately £23,000; this had to be spread over the three years, and we were fortunate to secure grant-aid from the Countryside Commission for that work.

The second problem was an outbreak of Beech Bark Disease, accentuated by the drought of 1976, which attacked many of the trees which had been planted on Lancelot Brown's instructions in the 1760s. In 1978–79, during the time when we were concentrating on the replanting of the Grand Avenue, a major problem arose with the eastern beech belt. Some years previously parts of the screen of trees in this area had been taken out and replanted, with a view to attempting to replant the whole belt in pieces and sections, so that in the long term its continuity would be secured; however, this piecemeal approach was overtaken by the more serious problems caused by the accelerating impact of Beech Bark Disease. It became necessary to fell almost all the beech trees in that area, from the Ditchley Gate to a point almost midway down the eastern park boundary. A considerable amount of replanting has already been carried out, in conjunction with the Countryside Commission and West Oxfordshire

District Council. However, it was becoming increasingly clear that the accelerated loss of beech was going to have a serious effect upon the landscape. As a result of discussions held with the Countryside Commission, the idea of an overall plan for the park emerged. The Commission agreed to grant-aid the provision of a plan, without the estate being placed in the position of having to carry out a decade or so of tree-planting before receiving full reimbursement of its costs.

After considerable research and consultation in connection with this proposal, His Grace appointed Ralph Cobham and Hal Moggridge as a combined consultancy to look at the whole question of the park and its restoration. His Grace is to be complimented on the initiative which he has taken towards the formulation of this plan, and for my part it was fascinating to have had a professional role in the teamwork involved in implementing it.

The Landscape Restoration Plan

Ralph Cobham

The brief drawn up jointly by His Grace, Paul Hutton and the Countryside Commission required the preparation of a restoration plan which would direct the future development of the park landscape. In particular, it was required that the plan would accommodate the retention (and, where necessary, restoration) of the historic aspects of the landscape, alongside the efficient performance of its modern functions of farming, forestry, shooting and tourism. Landscape objectives and land use priorities would be determined through the study of the park's historic, aesthetic, ecological and functional values. The landscape restoration plan would need to reflect these aims in a practical, aesthetically pleasing and co-ordinated, but flexible, manner. It should, therefore, aim to blend the old and the new, respecting the historic integrity of the old, while guiding and inspiring the new. By any standards this was a daunting task.

The approach adopted was to begin by analysing what might be termed the 'good' or 'asset' features of this landscape, and also its deficiencies and vulnerabilities. Hal Moggridge has already described this part of the work, based on documentary records and assessment of the aesthetic qualities of the present landscape. I want to go on to discuss the analysis of those assets and deficiencies from a functional point of view – that of land use, including nature conservation. The most significant task was to analyse the source of the problem. It would be all too easy to treat the immediate symptoms of the illness without finding its cause, and arriving at a solution which could be entirely inappropriate; a lasting cure and a successful long-term restoration policy depend on a correct identification of all the causes of the present difficulties.

One of the problems which was immediately recognisable was the poor age structure of the trees on the estate: between 50 and 55 per cent of the dedicated woodland cover on the estate is likely to require felling in the next twenty to twenty-five years. In short, there are too many old trees and not nearly enough young trees. The difficulty which faces us, then, is how to achieve a more varied age structure, while respecting the historic and aesthetic considerations of Brown's design which, ironically, is itself one of the origins of the problem. As has been amply demonstrated, Brown was a great artist, engineer and creator; nonetheless, he has suffered the fate experienced by so many great men, namely that his success already contained the potential seeds of its own demise. Possibly the supreme motive underlying Brown's work was an unquestioning confidence in the future. In his day enlightened patrons, backed by large fortunes, were able to support the vast retinue of estate staff, gardeners and labourers required to undertake the most daunting of physical operations. The supply of physical resources and of horticultural and silvicultural expertise must have seemed so natural at the time that the necessity of questioning how to perpetuate the Blenheim landscape, let alone of prescribing plans for it, was obviously of no great consequence. In that respect Brown, and some of his contemporaries and successors, were overconfident; unable to foresee changes in economic and social conditions, they left no indications of how they envisaged the replacement or succession of their plantings should be undertaken. It would be unfair to criticise them in this

122. Rotation of clumps: plantings by Brown (foreground) and the ninth Duke.
123. Young beeches planted before the Restoration Plan block one of Brown's vistas.

respect, but it should serve as a reminder to us not to overlook long-term needs in future.

One person, namely the ninth Duke, did understand the problem, and, as David Green and Hal Moggridge have shown, he acted accordingly around the turn of the century. It is worth quoting from the ninth Duke's Red Planting Record Book an entry made in 1900:

'It is clear that at the time when the House was built and for fifty years subsequently, extensive planting operations were carried out in the Park. Those persons who instituted the planting of trees at Blenheim understood the art, and the effect on the landscape which they desired to create, to a degree in which subsequent generations have been conspicuously deficient . . . The Old Park, where the Oaks and Bracken exist, was meant to remain as an example to all time of the imposing effect of a medieval forest. In a similar way, the monument in Low Park, where the elms were planted in avenues, was meant to convey to the observer the idea of style at the age of Queen Anne and of the 18th century, the period when the house was built. It has been my aim, in all the planting that I have given orders to be carried out, to preserve the foregoing peculiarities and characteristics of Blenheim Park. I have examined with regret the results of the planting carried out by those who were responsible for the arrangement of trees during the nineteenth century: they are arranged in an aimless fashion, and it appears as if this important subject has been left to the caprice of incompetent foresters or the will of unintelligent estate agents'.

This was indeed a pretty damning indictment.

Two years earlier, in 1898, referring to the High Park, he wrote:

'By planting these specimen oaks in every open spot I hope to preserve the effect of this forest of the Middle Ages. It appears to me that no oak has been planted in it for at least 150 years, which is a great pity. Many of the old oaks are dying, and if the planting of young ones is neglected the forest will soon cease to exist, except for the existence of a few old stumps. The planting of oak in the High Park should be continued for another 25 years and then the park will be stocked for 500 years to come'.

Although the ninth Duke's view of the frequency of rotational planting required in the oak woodland may have been somewhat awry, he, more than Brown or anyone else before his time, did appreciate something of the magnitude of the task involved in perpetuating what is essentially a living work of art. Nonetheless, to talk of planting for twenty-five years in the High Park and then allowing nature to take its course was unrealistic, and it

BLENHEIM PARK
LAND USES, 1982

Arable rotation land
Grazing land
Dedicated woodland
Canary grass/ Game crop
Area of highest ecological value
R   Permanent release pen
→   Main drives
D   Duck shooting : main stand
S   Sports pitches
......   Miniature railway tracks

Pleasure Grounds

Ancient
Oakwood

N

0   1 km

0   1 mile

124.   Blenheim Park: modern land utilisation.

is this attitude which has, in many ways, bedevilled the Blenheim landscape. Conservation here, as in the case of other historic parks, is not achieved simply by drawing a plan, carrying out a sort of blitzkrieg operation based on planting up again once and for all, and then forgetting all about it for another couple of centuries until the cycle is repeated. Instead, the treatment required more resembles the painting of the Forth Bridge, namely continuing and rotating attention to small parts of the whole. The problems we face today are (i) that for quite a long time too little has been done, (ii) in some places the wrong things have been done, and (iii) the difficulties have been accelerated by old age and by the misfortunes of disease.

Much has been said about the very important aesthetic aspects, but it must be remembered that in the present century this is also a working landscape, and it is necessary for the estate to earn money from its different departments in terms of the overall corporate plan.

Figure 124 shows the current land use within the park. It includes areas of dedicated woodland, the belts of trees around the eastern, northern and western margins of the park, and more especially, in the south-west and south. Arable land predominates in the northern part of the park, with smaller areas on the south-eastern side towards Bladon. Permanent pasture flanks the Grand Avenue and occupies much of the Low Park area. It is against this background that future management has to be planned and potential conflicts of interest resolved, and some of those interests should now be considered.

i. *Nature Conservation*. The High Park in the south-western quarter, the remnants of the oakwood/rough pasture landscape of the medieval deer park, is of major importance from the point of view of nature conservation. It is especially valuable for its range of lichens, bryophytes and invertebrates, and it has been designated by the Nature Conservancy Council (N.C.C.) as part of a Site of Special Scientific Interest (S.S.S.I.). Parts of this area have come under threat in the past from commercial reafforestation, and also from forms of management which have encouraged sycamore invasion; but improved liason with the staff of the N.C.C. has done much to resolve these difficulties.

A second parkland feature of importance in this respect is the lakes, where many wildfowl breed regularly and other species overwinter.

ii. *Agriculture*. The farming interests predominate in the northern half, the Great Park, and also in the south-east in the Lower Park and Bladon Park. From the farming angle, the peripheral screen of trees was valued as a shelter-belt, particularly that on the western side, and the perpetuation of this feature would be welcomed. However, because agricultural land is valuable, it was requested that any land taken for additional tree planting should be kept down to an absolute minimum. The practice of leaving lots of old tree stumps in permanent pasture was not popular, and their removal wherever possible was much to be desired. Thus some fairly strong guidelines were available from the farming interests. However, their requirements were not found to be severely in conflict with any of the other aspects.

iii. *Forestry*. Another important aspect of the estate's economy is its forestry department. Blenheim runs its own sawmill, and the forestry enterprise is expected, within the Park and within the estate as a whole, to show an economic return. Commercial forestry involving conifers rather than native hardwoods has become an inevitable fact of modern life, though its impact upon the park would probably have been regretted by the ninth Duke. The three principal problems facing the forestry department are delayed felling, delayed thinning or under-thinning, again a result of past neglect; and the estate is clearly foregoing a certain amount of commercial return as a direct result of those deficiencies. This stems directly from the fact that the management of the woodlands has tended in the past to be dominated by the sporting interests, thereby causing conflict. The forestry department was asked to put forward its own suggestions for new planting purely on a commercial basis, in order to assess how far this could be reconciled with other interests. They recommended afforestation alongside the western belt in the north-eastern part, and hoped for a substantial new area of coniferous planting adjoining an already large conifer plantation in the south-western quarter established in the 1950s and 60s, which unfortunately was in the middle of the S.S.S.I. This second proposal, therefore, had to be rejected.

iv. *Game*. The sporting interests have been especially important in recent decades, and this is to a large extent the reason for the retention of woodlands which should ideally have been felled and replanted in rotation years ago, for the delay of thinning, and for some new plantings which are inappropriate from the standpoint of both forestry and amenity. Ironically the existing woodlands have become increasingly unsatisfactory for sporting purposes, because they now lack the desirable warm understorey or shrub layer to provide a suitable habitat for the pheasants. Thinning can only be carried out in a period of six weeks between the end of the shooting season and the beginning of the next year's rearing programme. While many of the existing woodlands do need replacement, they have had to be retained as game cover until alternatives can be provided elsewhere. The game department, asked to produce its own ideal management requirements, looked for new woodland planting areas into which the forestry operation could be steered, and drew up its own recommendations for selective felling in the Lince area and phased replanting over a twenty-year period along the western shelter-belt. Some of the areas recommended for planting by the game department again proved unacceptable because of their encroachment over the S.S.S.I.

v. *Recreation.* Over 350,000 visitors come to Blenheim every year, and catering for leisure is today the most profitable single enterprise on the estate. This alone is sufficient justification for attempting to preserve and sustain the aesthetic qualities of the landscape; for if the scenery which attracts visitors to Blenheim decays, that very important revenue will decline correspondingly.

Any future management plan, then, needs to accommodate all of these interests and, over a period of time, to work as far as possible towards reconciling the conflicts between them and devising compromises which will allow the efficient operation of the revenue-earning functions while still respecting the historic, aesthetic and ecological aspects. The park was, therefore, divided into eight separate zones on the basis of aesthetic, land use and management values (fig. 125):

1. The Great Park, comprising the northern agricultural area, with its shelter-belt, avenue and other clumps.

2. The centrepiece of Lancelot Brown's design around the main lakes and the palace, where the buildings, the massing of trees on the banks of the lake, and the picturesque views through open spaces are important.

3. The two western tributary dry valleys, the Icehouse Valley to the north and the Combe Valley to the south, where the valley floor is open but clumps occupy the valley sides and the skyline along the edge of the plateau is important seen from below. Brown's landscaping filters into these areas without a sharp break from Zone 2, so they too are important from an aesthetic standpoint.

4. The High Park, the area of ancient oakwood with its glades and distant views, of special importance historically and ecologically.

5. The Pleasure Grounds south of the Palace with their ornamental and exotic trees and shrubs, walks, temples, cascade and other features beyond Duchêne's formal gardens; this area is not significantly affected by the management plan.

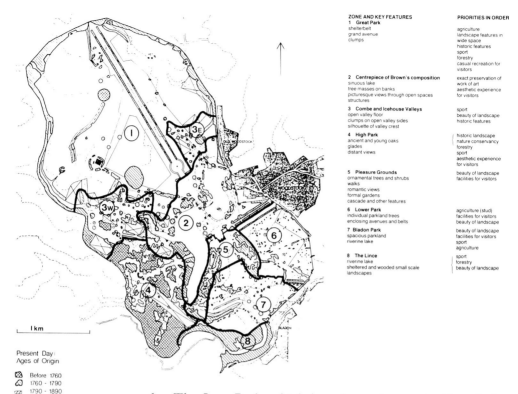

ZONE AND KEY FEATURES
1 Great Park
shelterbelt
grand avenue
clumps

PRIORITIES IN ORDER
agriculture
landscape features in
wide space
historic features
sport
forestry
casual recreation for
visitors

2 Centrepiece of Brown's composition
sinuous lake
tree masses on banks
picturesque views through open spaces
structures

exact preservation of
work of art
aesthetic experience
for visitors

3 Combe and Icehouse Valleys
open valley floor
clumps on open valley sides
silhouette of valley crest

sport
beauty of landscape
historic features

4 High Park
ancient and young oaks
glades
distant views

historic landscape
nature conservancy
forestry
sport
aesthetic experience
for visitors

5 Pleasure Grounds
ornamental trees and shrubs
walks
romantic views
formal gardens
cascade and other features

beauty of landscape
facilities for visitors

6 Lower Park
individual parkland trees
enclosing avenues and belts

agriculture (stud)
facilities for visitors
beauty of landscape

7 Bladon Park
spacious parkland
riverine lake

beauty of landscape
facilities for visitors
sport
agriculture

8 The Lince
riverine lake
sheltered and wooded small scale
landscapes

sport
forestry
beauty of landscape

1 km

Present Day:
Ages of Origin

Before 1760
1760 - 1790
1790 - 1890
1890 - 1935
Since 1935

125.   The zoning plan.

6.   The Low Park, which has changed very significantly in character in recent years, largely because of the present Duke's interest in establishing a stud farm there, so that although a few clumps of trees may be desirable to provide shade, they are not required on the scale provided in Wise's plan which had been allowed to remain intact by Brown.

7.   Bladon Park, of rather different character to the other parkland areas to the north, with some areas of arable farming encroaching over it, but remaining primarily pastoral, the area being on an altogether smaller scale than the vast open plateau to the north. The riverine lake below the cascade is an important aesthetic component.

8.   The Lince, that delightful small landscape devised by Brown in the lowest part of the park, with its own part of the riverine lake and its intimate sheltered woodland character.

It was clearly not appropriate to envisage some sweeping restoration plan for the whole park; instead, it was necessary to look more carefully at each of these component zones and to devise something suited to their own individual characters and functions.

Each zone may have to satisfy the needs, not just of one, but

SURVEYS, ANALYSES AND PLANS

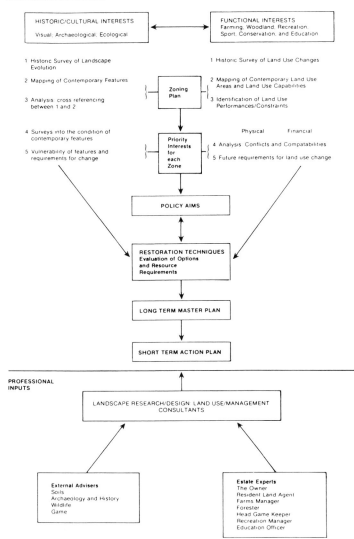

| HISTORIC/CULTURAL INTERESTS | | FUNCTIONAL INTERESTS |
| Visual; Archaeological; Ecological | | Farming, Woodland, Recreation, Sport, Conservation, and Education |

1 Historic Survey of Landscape Evolution

2 Mapping of Contemporary Features

3 Analysis: cross referencing between 1 and 2

Zoning Plan

1 Historic Survey of Land Use Changes

2 Mapping of Contemporary Land Use Areas and Land Use Capabilities

3 Identification of Land Use Performances/Constraints

4 Surveys into the condition of contemporary features

5 Vulnerability of features and requirements for change

Priority Interests for each Zone

Physical   Financial

4 Analysis: Conflicts and Compatabilities

5 Future requirements for land use change

POLICY AIMS

RESTORATION TECHNIQUES
Evaluation of Options
and Resource
Requirements

LONG TERM MASTER PLAN

SHORT TERM ACTION PLAN

PROFESSIONAL INPUTS

LANDSCAPE RESEARCH/DESIGN LAND USE/MANAGEMENT
CONSULTANTS

External Advisers
Soils
Archaeology and History
Wildlife
Game

Estate Experts
The Owner
Resident Land Agent
Farms Manager
Forester
Head Game Keeper
Recreation Manager
Education Officer

126. The processes involved in producing the Landscape Restoration Plan.

of a number of land uses and a number of functions; however, for most of the zones it is possible to set a priority function towards which management and restoration policies must be aimed, while still accommodating, so far as is possible, other desirable functions. In the northern zone, the Great Park, agriculture should continue to be the primary land use. In Brown's centrepiece around the lake it is obviously the aesthetic aspects, geared towards the enjoyment and satisfaction of visitors, which must come first. In the Combe Valley and Icehouse Valley the sporting interests predominate, though, because these areas are part of the landscaping work of both Brown and the ninth Duke, the preservation of their scenic beauty is also extremely important. In the High Park, the remains of the medieval forest, nature conservation takes priority, with aesthetics also being important. The very nature of the Pleasure Grounds south of the Palace dictates that they should continue to be managed primarily for the enjoyment of visitors. In the Lower Park agriculture and the stud farm take priority. In Bladon Park the aesthetic aspects and the recreation of visitors will continue to be the dominant needs. Finally, the Lince is extremely valuable for sport and for forestry, but also has a significant aesthetic aspect, although at present this is not accessible for the enjoyment of the public, apart from an occasional school party.

Before the specifics of the restoration plan could be drawn up, overall policy aims had to be set. Five principal objectives were established:

i.   To conserve in perpetuity the key aesthetic features of Capability Brown's masterpiece, also maintaining the sense of continuity and alternation initiated by the ninth Duke as closely as possible.

ii.   To conserve all the other important historic features, the archaeological sites and ancient earthworks, the medieval open oakwood, the avenues and clumps.

iii.   To ensure that the contemporary land uses are integrated in a manner complementary to the historic park.

iv.   To maintain the distinctive character of each of the eight defined zones, where necessary removing existing features which have the effect of blurring their character.

v.   To provide a long-term plan as a basis for landscape perpetuation, in particular to avoid a recurrence of the situation whereby a predominance of old trees demands clear-felling in large blocks; recognising that beech has a maximum life of only 200–250 years, and oak possibly twice as long as that, a scheme to achieve a varied age structure of the trees in the park is essential.

The restoration approach involves essentially three techniques leading towards a balanced tree structure:

i.   Natural regeneration, where nature effectively takes care of the job itself, may be possible in parts of the High Park in years of good acorn production. Clearly there are many self-sown oak saplings here which will contribute to the next generation of trees, and these will require special protection during their early years of life.

ii.   Continuous replacement, a technique involving selective felling and replanting in small areas or pockets, will be appropriate for some of the larger woodland blocks, where the aim is to attempt to maintain the profile of the feature in perpetuity, with a full spectrum of age-ranges from young saplings to large trees past their maturity.

iii.   Sequential replanting of smaller features where continuous replacement is not possible, such as avenues and clumps. This technique involves planting young understudy tree groups approximately halfway through the life of the existing feature, the idea being that the understudies will have grown to maturity by the time the original feature needs to be clear-felled. Thus there is an alternation or rotation of clumps and avenues, so that the key features are always in existence in the landscape at any one time, though in one of two alternative specific locations.

In addition incidental planting will be required in appropriate areas throughout the decade, though it is important that this should not be done in a capricious or *ad hoc* manner.

The Master Plan

The main components of the restoration envisaged will be as follows:

i.   In the western and eastern perimeter belts and several other large features, restoration using the continuous replacement technique is proposed. There will, undoubtedly, be problems with this approach initially. In the western belt

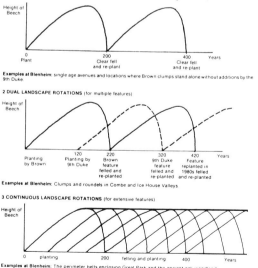

127.   Approaches to landscape restoration.

particularly, there is some doubt whether there is room enough to achieve the desired effect, and the situation there is such that within about twenty to thirty-five years probably no mature trees will survive.

ii.   In the High Park natural regeneration of the oaks is to be encouraged on a continuing basis.

iii.   The round clumps in the Great Park will require clear-felling on a 60–110 year rotation, using beech, chestnut and lime. In the Icehouse Valley and Combe Valley, fortunately, because of the enlightened contribution of the ninth Duke some 120–140 years after Brown's original plantations, the basis for such a rotation already exists in part. The Fourteen-Acre Clump, between the Combe Valley and the Grand Avenue, ironically, has suffered by virtue of becoming a mixed-age clump: when the centre needed felling, it was replanted with a mixture of larch and beech. This has yet to be thinned, and to maintain the effect of visual continuity the outer perimeter of beech was retained. In itself, this was an excellent thing to have done, but unfortunately the beech suffered severely in the years of drought. The problem now is, should the beech be felled prematurely rather than being allowed to fall down, and should it then be replanted in an attempt to have the outer rim of beech established by the time that the larch in the centre is thinned and removed, so that the whole clump can then grow on together? Management of a mixed-age clump of this type is very awkward. Further north, in the agricultural part of the Great Park, there are four smaller clumps of similar age – should we be brave and fell one of these clumps prematurely, in order to put the rotation cycle into operation? One of these clumps at present is still effectively fenced against livestock, but the others are either unfenced or surrounded by fences which have not

128.   Restoration planting on the approach to the palace from the Woodstock gate. Parked cars create a serious visual intrusion on the dramatic series of views designed along this approach.

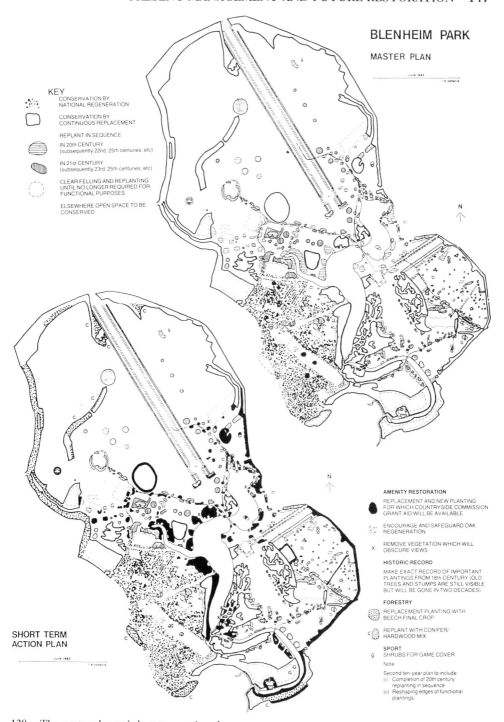

BLENHEIM PARK

MASTER PLAN

June 1982

KEY
CONSERVATION BY
NATIONAL REGENERATION

CONSERVATION BY
CONTINUOUS REPLACEMENT

REPLANT IN SEQUENCE

IN 20th CENTURY
(subsequently 22nd, 25th centuries, etc)

IN 21st CENTURY
(subsequently 23rd, 25th centuries, etc)

CLEAR FELLING AND REPLANTING
UNTIL NO LONGER REQUIRED FOR
FUNCTIONAL PURPOSES

ELSEWHERE OPEN SPACE TO BE
CONSERVED

N

N

SHORT TERM
ACTION PLAN

June 1982

AMENITY RESTORATION

REPLACEMENT AND NEW PLANTING
FOR WHICH COUNTRYSIDE COMMISSION
GRANT AID WILL BE AVAILABLE

ENCOURAGE AND SAFEGUARD OAK
REGENERATION

X   REMOVE VEGETATION WHICH WILL
OBSCURE VIEWS

HISTORIC RECORD

MAKE EXACT RECORD OF IMPORTANT
PLANTINGS FROM 18th CENTURY (OLD
TREES AND STUMPS ARE STILL VISIBLE
BUT WILL BE GONE IN TWO DECADES)

FORESTRY

REPLACEMENT PLANTING WITH
BEECH FINAL CROP

C   REPLANT WITH CONIFER/
HARDWOOD MIX

SPORT

G   SHRUBS FOR GAME COVER

Note

Second ten-year plan to include
(i)   Completion of 20th century
      replanting in sequence
(ii) Reshaping edges of functional
      plantings

129.   The master plan and short-term action plan.

been maintained, so that livestock have gained access for shelter and shade, and natural regeneration has been prevented. The success of the overall grand restoration plan will depend upon the resolution of such mundane technical problems.

iv.   The existing Grand Avenue, planted with limes in the late 1970s, will obviously require replanting in the twenty-second and twenty-fourth centuries, and the Master Plan recommends the planting of a second avenue, outside and parallel to the existing rows, in the twenty-first century, to be replaced in the twenty-third and twenty-fifth centuries and in successive centuries thereafter. It had been hoped that, because of the precedent set by both Wise and the ninth Duke, it would be possible to reintroduce some sort of centrepiece to the Grand Avenue, and to build in the same sort of rotation there; but this has not been accepted as a top priority.

Within the Master Plan there is a ten- to fifteen-year short-term action plan upon which we are already embarked, which involves some amenity replanting with Countryside Commission grant-aid, the positive encouragement of oak regeneration in the High Park, the removal of intrusive veget-ation which obscures important views, and some commercial forestry plantations with both conifers and hardwoods, also the provision of shrub cover for game birds. In the following section Paul Hutton will describe what has been achieved in the first year.

Restoration in Action: The First Year

Paul Hutton

Given the existence of the master plan and our awareness of the problems, the next step was to look at the first year's planting and to establish the priorities. The work on the estate was divided into two categories, firstly the work which was grant-aided by the Countryside Commission, comprising essentially the planting which was regarded as critical for the amenity aspects of the landscape, and secondly that which has been supported by the Forestry Commission grant-aid scheme; and, in order to obtain the maximum financial support, we have divided our plan on that basis. The Forestry Officer of West Oxfordshire District Council, Matthew O'Brien, has also played a very active part in the work.

One of our most immediate problems was one of the belts in Old Woodstock, where some mature beeches survived, but with a lot of gaps. One of the original ideas was to plant out circles within the existing trees, and some time was spent in examining this option and the potential extent of the circles, before it was realised that many of them would be in danger of coalescing. Eventually it was decided to fence off the whole of the belt, and to begin planting new trees behind the fence.

A second area to receive attention was the road down to the Cowyards in the area where the bloodstock is maintained. As has been indicated in earlier papers, the Low Park was very heavily populated with trees into the mid-1950s, but has since become more and more open. A new avenue has now been planted along the Cowyards road in order to break this up a little. Small trees have been bought in and nurtured on the estate until they have reached an appropriate height, and with each tree costing perhaps £20, they have had to be protected against both cattle and people.

A further area of new plantation has been on Bladon Bank, and care has been taken in this area to leave a gap in the middle in order to maintain the vista.

On the very southern edge of the park, in the area known as the Nursery, where nursery tree stocks were formerly kept, we have been able to establish a new belt in between the gnarled and beautiful old oak trees, primarily with beech, along part of the boundary which previously had no substantial belt around it.

Another part of the park boundary which previously had no perimeter belt but which has now been planted up is in the Cowyards area. There is a caravan site immediately outside the wall at this point, and while the caravans are an important source of income to the estate, they do inevitably detract somewhat from the landscape. In future, however, they will be screened from within the park when the newly-planted trees have grown up sufficiently.

130. The new avenue to the Cowyards;
131. Replanting in the north-east shelter belt.

Restoration in Action: The Immediate Future

Ralph Cobham

The top priority for next year's work and for successive years must now be the centrepiece zone of Brown's planting, and Hal Moggridge will be working out very carefully which particular views and vistas are to be opened up, involving the removal of some existing features, both old and young. One of the vistas in particular, that linking High Lodge with the palace, has become seriously obscured through natural regeneration, and one of the main pieces of work will be simply to keep nature at bay there, so that the ride can be enjoyed by people looking out from Duchêne's terrace garden.

Finally, and most importantly, quite a lot of selective felling has been undertaken along the western perimeter belt. If the trees here had been left much longer, the cost of felling and clearing would have been simply astronomical, and at least by felling now while there was still some timber value in the trees, some of their felling costs have been recouped. So, again, this will be a prime target for planting this coming autumn.

A restoration plan on a site so vast and complex as Blenheim is an immense undertaking, made the more challenging by the need to reconcile so many different interests. Almost any scheme which could have been devised would have been bound to contain its controversial elements and its periods when not much, or too much, seemed to be happening. However, we believe that a basis has now been established, both for the efficient functioning of the various interests within the estate economy, and for the perpetuation of a landscape which can continue to be enjoyed by generations to come.

Bibliography

COBHAM R. 1984: 'Blenheim: The Art and Management of Landscape Restoration', *Landscape Research* Vol. 9 No. 2, pp. 4–14, and reprinted in *Arboricultural Jnl.* Vol. 9 No. 2 (1985), pp. 81–99.

COBHAM R. & HUTTON P. 1983: 'Brown in Memoriam: Blenheim in Perpetuity', *Landscape Design* No. 146.

GIBBS J.N. & GREIG B.J.W. 1977: 'Some Consequences of the 1975–6 Drought for Dutch Elm Disease in Southern England', *Forestry* Vol. 50, pp. 145–54.

GREEN J. 1982: 'Parkland and Agriculture', *Landscape Research* Vol. 7 No. 1, pp. 23–24.

GREIG B.J.W. 1981: 'The History of the Elm Avenues at Blenheim and Dutch Elm Disease', *Quarterly Journal of Forestry* Vol. 75 No. 4.

MOGGRIDGE H.T. 1983: 'Blenheim Park: the Restoration Plan', *Landscape Design* No. 146.

WORKMAN G. 1982: 'Restoration of Parklands and Subsequent Management', *Landscape Research* Vol. 7 No. 1, pp. 29–30.

WRIGHT T.W.J. 1982: *Large Gardens and Parks: Maintenance, Management and Design* (Granada, London).

12. INTO THE NEXT MILLENNIUM

Philip Everett and Kate Tiller

'By 1981, it was recognised that the core of the Park landscape, Brown's composition of tree masses and structures set against green sward and water, had become fragile with age.'[1]

THIS FRAGILITY was a major spur to the master plan for the restoration and future management of the Park referred to in Chapter 11. The national and international importance of the man-made landscape of Blenheim, to be reinforced by its designation as a World Heritage Site by ICOMOS (International Council on Monuments and Sites) in 1987, was more than ever apparent. It was equally clear that the resources and expertise so much taken for granted by Capability Brown in the 1770s (see p. 136) could not be assumed in the very different climate of the 1980s. Thus the thinking behind the master plan and its subsequent implementation had to combine not only a most valuable recording and analysis of the historical evidence of land use and physical features but also an assessment of the working functions of the Park within the late twentieth-century estate economy of Blenheim. These functions proved multifarious – aesthetic, historic and ecological factors, agriculture, forestry, countryside sports and game, tourism, recreation and education. They are encapsulated in the zoning plan of the Park (fig. 125) which has remained a major reference point for all subsequent management decisions.

Out of this recording and assessment emerged the overall objectives (p. 144) and the specific tasks planned (pp. 145-8) for the foreseeable future. The conference papers published in 1987 reflected these plans just one year after their formulation. 1996 marks the end of the first fifteen-year action plan for the restoration and management of Blenheim Park and was the occasion for a detailed review of progress so far and for renewed planning for the future. This chapter will look at what happened during those first fifteen years, how (if at all) that experience has affected the master plan, and at future prospects and aims.

Restoration in Action: The First Fifteen Years

Each year, in July or August, those involved in drawing up the overall plans for Blenheim Park, the Land Agent, Ralph Cobham and Hal Moggridge, meet to review the past year's progress and to look at plans for the coming year.[2] This scheme of work is drawn up with reference to the original master plan and, following approval by the Duke of Marlborough, is the basis for work undertaken on the estate, particularly by the Head Forester and his staff, during the subsequent three to six months.

Inevitably the best laid long-term plans can be disrupted by unforeseen factors. During the period 1981-1996 Blenheim experienced its fair share of tempest and pestilence. The violent storms of 1987 and 1990, severe summer droughts, continuing tree disease (beech bark necrosis and Dutch elm disease) and problems with predators have all played their part. Grey squirrels have proved a particular threat to beech trees up to twenty years old, which, being shallow rooted, have also suffered in drought conditions. The overall vulnerability of beeches, both young and old, has led to modifications in the original plans. Now no old beech tree, even if distorted by gale damage or senility, is to be felled other than for safety reasons. Continuous replanting will be undertaken as necessary and consideration will be given to diversifying species planted, until the longer-term fate of beeches at Blenheim is clearer. Alternatives, in recreating a sense of mass in the landscape, are Spanish chestnuts or sycamores.

Other external agents of change include the economic climate. Despite the recession of the 1980s visitor numbers have not declined and now run at over 800,000 per year. The business of managing public access, particularly to the central area of Brown's landscape around the Palace, therefore remains of prime importance. The levels of restoration work are also related to the availability of grants; thus in the aftermath of the gales help for replanting was available through the Task Force Tree scheme, whilst under the Set Aside arrangements some farming land use within the Park has been changed on a rotational basis. Elsewhere the Woodland Grant Scheme, Forestry Enterprise and English Heritage grants have been involved in aspects of the landscape restoration.

Technological changes were judged by the recent review of the restoration plan to account for 'the distinct visual impression that the Park has a more manicured appearance in 1996 than fifteen years earlier'. A combination of factors, including improvements in agrochemicals, in their more selective use, and changes in machinery, is thought to account for this trend.

Given the aims of the original plan and the impact of these external factors, what has happened to Blenheim Park in the last fifteen years?

Priority has been given to the 'centrepiece' of the Park, the area of Brown's landscape around the lake and the Palace. Here precise restoration, involving thinning and exact shaping, is being undertaken to ensure sightlines, open spaces and clumps as in

Brown's design. Stands of pure beech at four metre distances were planted. This 'purist' approach means that in the 'centrepiece' area some trees planted in the 'wrong' place for the Brown design have been felled. Work has started on reopening visual links between the Palace and the High Lodge area, thus linking the formal areas of landscape to the natural, wilderness areas. It is planned to pursue this theme further. However, because of the distress to beeches mentioned above, this technique had to be modified and plantings now include a precautionary intermixing of species. The clear felling of whole areas is being avoided, and ancient trees retained as long as possible. The policy is one of continuous replacement, with an uneven age structure of trees. Away from the 'centrepiece', in the Great Park, in Combe and Icehouse Valleys, in Bladon Park and the Lince, a longer-term policy of deliberately intermixed planting is being followed.

In the Great Park plantings in the east and west perimeter belts are growing very rapidly and major thinning in the eastern belt will need to be undertaken. This is an example of the need to strike a balance between continuing new work on the one hand and the maintenance requirements of recent plantings on the other – a major consideration in a situation where 15,700 trees have been planted in the fifteen-year period and some 30 hectares of woodland copse and game covers under- or replanted.

An interesting instance of the balance between functional and aesthetic considerations has arisen over the plantings of belts in the Great Park. In order 'to relieve the tedium of continuing uniformity' the proposals to soften the edges of such belts by shrub planting, thus creating the illusion of an irregular field boundary, have been reinforced.

Also in the Great Park the erection of extensive new farm buildings at Park Farm has raised further restoration issues. The farm, and its surrounding shelter plantation, were part of Brown's original layout for the Park. By 1982 the shelter belt was partially derelict and various buildings have subsequently been added to the north of the existing farmyard. The decision was taken to meet both practical and aesthetic pressures by creating a new shelter belt, emulating Brown's original feature but located to the north of the original in order to take in the new buildings. In such cases the restoration plan has informed practical solutions to present-day problems. The hope is that the results preserve the spirit of the eighteenth-century landscape.

In addition to Brown's 'centrepiece' and the Great Park, a third major area of concern during the 1981-1996 period has been the High Park, the area of ancient oak woodland. Here a policy of encouraging natural regeneration rather than replanting has been

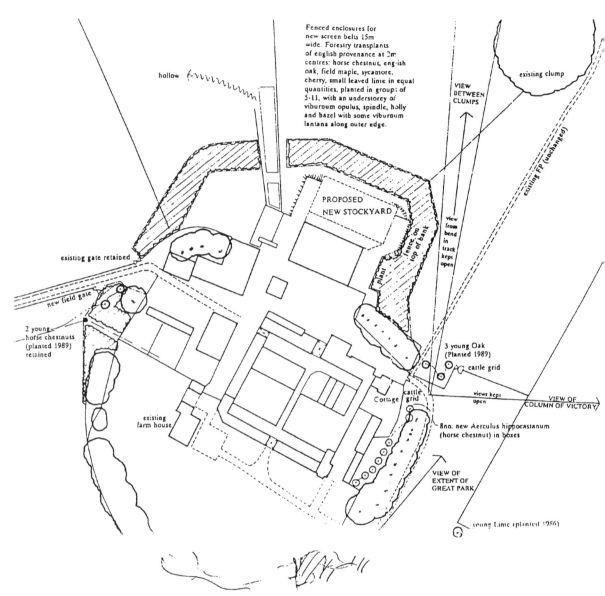

Fenced enclosures for new screen belts 15m wide. Forestry transplants of english provenance at 2m centres: horse chestnut, english oak, field maple, sycamore, cherry, small leaved lime in equal quantities, planted in groups of 5-11, with an understorey of viburnum opulus, spindle, holly and hazel with some viburnum lantana along outer edge.

hollow

VIEW BETWEEN CLUMPS

existing clump

existing FP (unchanged)

PROPOSED NEW STOCKYARD

view from bend in track kept open

plant fence on top of bank

existing gate retained

new field gate

2 young horse chestnuts (planted 1989) retained

3 young Oak (Planted 1989)

cattle grid

Cottage

cattle grid

views kept open

VIEW OF COLUMN OF VICTORY

existing farm house

8no. new Aerculus hippocastanum (horse chestnut) in boxes

VIEW OF EXTENT OF GREAT PARK

young Lime (planted 1986)

132. At Park Farm in the Great Park both modern and historic considerations have been taken into account. New screening belts, in emulation of Brown, have been planted but located to take in new farm buildings.[3]

adopted. Senile and fallen oaks have been left *in situ* to sustain food chains whilst young, self-seeded oaks have been protected by tree shelters and guards. This management policy has also been beneficial to game. English Nature have undertaken a number of surveys in the S.S.S.I. area.

The land use pattern in the Park has remained substantially the same as in 1981. Two areas of arable south of the Palace have been returned to permanent pasture. The use of fertilisers and chemicals in the Park has been modified. Some Set Aside has been adopted on a rotational basis. Cattle and sheep are grazed more extensively in the Great Park, with continuing problems of protection for trees.

Overall in the past fifteen years some 80 per cent of Blenheim Park has been restored in accordance with strategies based upon careful historic analysis. A series of judgements has had to be made about which era to favour in the restoration of individual items and about the extent to which adaptation to twentieth-century utility is appropriate. However, no more than 15 per cent of the Park has changed in character from its historic form and such changes have been consistent with the need to maintain overall coherence. Key areas have been the maintenance of the precise historic integrity of the core of the Park, of the spacious grandeur of the Great Park, and of the oakwood wilderness in High Park.

Detailed thinning, shaping and tree planting will be needed to perfect details of the restored landscape. Also there is a continuing need to integrate sporting improvements and aesthetic restoration. Much has been achieved but replanting cycles and ongoing maintenance of existing work will require continuous effort by the Estate staff throughout the Park on an annual basis.

Restoration in Action: Into the Next Millennium

The review of 1996 has confirmed the validity of the classification of the Park into eight zones. Thus they have served as the basis of a phase 2 action plan for 1996–2011. This proposes the continued adoption of the master plan with cyclical selective felling, replanting, some use of natural regeneration and consistent management on an annual basis.

Some modifications which evolved during phase 1, for example mixed age planting rather than clear felling, are recommended to be continued. Other themes will be the maintenance of structures, including the Grand Bridge, the Triumphal Arch and the lake and its dam. In the area of forestry the eventual felling of conifer plantations in the High Park area is included. The need to foster nature conservation under the Countryside Stewardship Scheme is recognised in the case of the farm dairies. This will involve modifying grassland management methods so that biodiversity is both conserved and enhanced. The creation of wildlife corridors also features in the proposals for the next ten to fifteen years. Another major aim is the planting of the outer two rows of the double Grand Avenue during the first twenty-five years of the twenty-first century, a monumental feature of the Park landscape indeed. Mundane but important will be the recurrent need for maintenance through weeding, thinning and felling. Finally it is hoped that visitors' appreciation and awareness of the richness and complexities of the Park landscape and features can be increased by interpretive material and displays.

References

1. Blenheim Estate Office with Scott Wilson Resource Consultants and Colvin and Moggridge, *Blenheim Park Landscape Restoration and Management. An action plan for phase 2, 1996-2011* (September 1996).
2. COBHAM, R. 'Preparation of Restoration Plans', in *Celebration of Trees* (Proceedings of the Arboricultural Association Conference, 1989).
3   Blenheim Estate Office, op. cit., A6.II.

13. SOME ASPECTS OF THE NATURAL HISTORY OF BLENHEIM PALACE

John Campbell

APART FROM bird-watching around the Queen Pool, the natural history of Blenheim Park has not been studied at all systematically. Casual visits by naturalists have indicated that the park has a rich fauna and flora, and would amply repay more detailed study. This paper is no more than a tentative review of our present state of knowledge.

Blenheim Park can be divided into several main types of habitat, which will be described below. These major habitats can in turn be subdivided many times, down to the level of such specialised habitats as the rotting red heart wood of the ancient oak trees, *Quercus robur*, or the various bracket fungi which grow upon the trees. Such micro-habitats all have their own specialised faunas, mostly flies and beetles.

Habitats

1. *The Park Grassland*

Large areas in the central part of the park consist of grazed grassland with scattered trees and clumps. It is this habitat which surrounds much of the palace, the Queen Pool and the Column of Victory. Most of the grassland is calcareous, and in places a variety of herbs, such as the Stemless Thistle (*Cirsium acaulon*), Rockrose (*Helianthemum chamaecistus*) and Harebell (*Campanula rotundifolia*), are to be found. The trees range from ancient Oaks (*Quercus robur*), through planted native species such as Beech (*Fagus sylvaticus*) to introduced species such as the various kinds of Cedar (*Cedrus* spp.). The grazing prevents the invasion of shrubs and trees into the grassland.

2. *Rough Herbage and Scrub*

Throughout the park there are areas of ungrazed and unmown herbage. In such places ranker growing species and shrubs prosper. Some areas are calcareous, and support the tall Woolly Thistle (*Cirsium eriopherum*) and the Deadly Nightshade (*Atropa belladonna*). Other regions are damper, with Marsh Thistle (*Carduus acanthoides*) and Great Willowherb (*Epilobium hirsutum*) usually well-represented. The scrub species range from Briar (*Rosa canina*) to Hawthorn (*Crataegus monogyna*) and Buckthorn (*Rhamnus cantharticus*). The berry-bearing shrubs are an important source of autumn and winter food for many birds.

3. *Woodlands*

The woodlands within the park are very varied, ranging from the ancient Oak (*Quercus robur*) woodland of the High Park in the vicinity of Combe Lodge, to post-war plantations of various species of conifers. Within the woodlands the soils vary, giving rise to different types of shrub and field layers.

The *conifer plantations* are mostly Larch (*Larix* spp.) and Pines (*Pinus* spp.), with smaller numbers of Spruce (*Picea* spp.) and other genera. Once these are well established, most other plants are shaded out. Birds such as the Coal Tit (*Parus ater*) and Goldcrest (*Regulus regulus*) favour the conifers, as do some ladybirds such as *Aphidecta obliterata* and *Chilocorus renipustulatus*.

The *broad-leaved woodland* is mixed, with areas of Ash (*Fraxinus excelsior*) saplings and patches of Common Elm (*Ulmus procera*) sprouting from the bases of trees killed by Dutch Elm Disease. Sometimes there is Sallow (*Salix* spp.) scrub as well as Hawthorn (*Crataegus monogyna*) in the shrub layer on the wetter soils. In other regions there is Bracken (*Pteridium aquilinium*) or various grasses.

The woodland of greatest interest is the area in the western part of the park which is dominated by the ancient Pedunculate Oaks (*Quercus robur*). Here the oldest trees, with girths ranging from 6·7–8·9m., are estimated to date from the early fifteenth century. These trees have been pollarded, and are now dying back at the tips of the branches. Some have partly hollow trunks, and represent a very special series of micro-habitats for some invertebrates. Between the oldest oaks there are standards with girths ranging from 4·8–5·8m., which may date back to the early eighteenth century. Scattered amongst these fine trees are much smaller standard oak trees about a hundred years of age.

4. *Aquatic Habitats*

The lakes, formed by damming the River Glyme, are a most striking feature and add a wide range of animal and plant life to the park. The Queen Pool is mostly very shallow, and in 1976, when the water level dropped by little more than 30cm, large areas of mud were exposed. The main lake below the Grand Bridge is very deep in places, whilst the Bladon Water below the Cascade is comparatively shallow. The margins of the lakes vary. In places there are beds of Bullrush (*Scirpus lacustris*) and Bur-reed (*Sparganium erectum*). Where mud and detritus collects in some of the small bays marsh plants such as Water Forget-me-Not (*Myosotis scorpoides*) and Tripartite Bur-marigold (*Bidens tripartita*) thrive. Near Rosamund's Well there

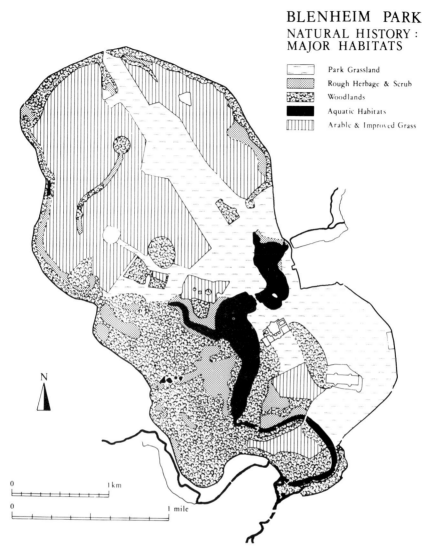

BLENHEIM PARK
NATURAL HISTORY :
MAJOR HABITATS

Park Grassland
Rough Herbage & Scrub
Woodlands
Aquatic Habitats
Arable & Improved Grass

133.   Natural history habitats in the park.

is a stretch of stony shallows, but much of the lake margins consist of fairly steep soil cliffs, plunging some 30 cm or so into the water, with little fringing vegetation. At the head of the lake, where it is entered by the River Glyme, there is a considerable amount of Flote-grass (*Glyceria* spp.)

There are some small pools near High Lodge and Mapleton Pond in the north-west of the park, which have not been investigated. In addition there are several streams and springs which give rise to wet flushes and marshy patches.

5. *Arable Land*

Quite a large area of the park is now cultivated, most of the crops being cereals. This habitat is transient, and now liberally treated with herbicides, pesticides and artificial fertilizer; it supports little wildlife.

Systematic Lists

The main groups of animals and plants represented in the park are reviewed below. As will be seen, the amount of information available is generally small. Most of the data used is held in file 62.76 of the Oxfordshire Biological Recording Scheme operated by Oxfordshire County Council Department of Museum Services.

Plants

1. *Lichens*

The lichen flora of the park has been recorded by Dr. H.J.M. Bowen (Bowen, 1980). Sixteen lichen species considered to be indicators of old woodland were recorded. Only Wychwood Forest has a greater total of such lichens in Oxfordshire. Wychwood was the only site in the three counties of Oxfordshire, Berkshire and Buckinghamshire to be categorised as 'good' for lichens; Blenheim, along with one other Oxfordshire site and single sites in the neighbouring two counties, was categorised as 'moderate'. Four of the indicator species present in Blenheim figure in the list of thirty lichens faithful to old woodland produced by Dr. F. Rose (Rose, 1976); only eleven of Rose's thirty species are known to occur anywhere in the three counties. The four present in Blenheim are indicated by an asterisk in the list below:

*Arthonia vinosa**	*Ochrolechia androgyna*
Calicium salicinum	*Opegrapha lyncea**
Cladonia parasitica	*Opegrapha rufescens*
*Enterographa crassa**	*Parmelia perlata*
Gyalecta truncigena	*Pertusaria flavida*
Lecanactis abietina	*Pertusaria hemisphaerica*
*Lecanactis premnea**	*Rinodina roboris*
Lecidea sublivescens	*Schismatomma niveum*

Another notable species, *Usnea hirta*, has not been recorded in Blenheim since 1928.

2. *Bryophytes*

In one visit in March 1982 Dr. E.W. Jones and G. Bloom recorded 90 species and varieties from the western part of the park. Amongst this total were a number of local species in Oxfordshire, such as *Brachythecium salebrosum, Bryum gemmiferum, Bryum klingsraeffii, Platygynium repens* and *Tortula virescens.*

3. *Other non-flowering plants*

Only a few casual records exist for fungi and other groups of non-flowering plants. It can be anticipated that fungi, especially those associated with dead and rotting wood, will be well-represented.

4. *Flowering plants*

A list of plants growing in the park is given in the 1811 edition of Mavor's *New Description of Blenheim.* Some of the plants listed by Mavor were undoubtedly introduced and naturalised, such as the Summer Snowflake (*Leucojum aestivum*) and Daffodil (*Narcissus* spp.). Others most probably once grew wild, but have since been lost, including the Fly Orchid (*Ophrys insectifera*) and Fragrant Orchid (*Gymnadenia conopsea*).

Several of the commoner flowering plants were mentioned in the description of the habitats above, and it is proposed here only to supplement these lists.

Additional calcareous grassland species include Thyme (*Thymus drucei*), Zigzag Clover (*Trifolium medium*), Wild Liquorice (*Astragalus glycyphyllos*) and Wild Parsnip (*Pastinaca sativa*). Travellers Joy (*Clematis vitalba*) grows again upon the more calcareous soils, while another climber, Woody Nightshade (*Solanum dulcamara*) is found in damper places.

The typical spring flowers of woodland, Primrose (*Primula vulgaris*), Wood Anemone (*Anemone nemorosa*) and drifts of Bluebells (*Endymion non-scriptus*) can be found. Later in the year the Greater Butterfly Orchid (*Plantathera chlorantha*) occurs beneath the beech trees.

Additional tree species include Hedge Maple (*Acer campestre*), Wych Elm (*Ulmus glabra*), Gean (*Prunus avium*), and Hornbeam (*Carpinus betulus*). Hazel (*Corylus avellana*), Spindle (*Euonymus europaeus*) and Purging Buckthorn (*Rhamnus catharticus*) all occur in the shrub layer.

The damp flushes in the open contain such species as Creeping Jenny (*Lysimachia nummularia*), Common Spotted Orchid (*Dactylorhiza fuchsii*) and, where it is more acidic, the Greater Birdsfoot Trefoil (*Lotus pedunculatus*).

A recent colonist has been the Himalayan Balsam (*Impatiens glandulifera*), which occurs where the River Glyme enters the head of Queen Pool.

A great deal of work is still required to obtain full lists of the flowering plants occurring throughout the park.

Animals

Only a limited amount of work has been done on the fauna, with the exception of the birds. Nonetheless, despite the small amount of data, specialist sampling has led to Blenheim Park being noted as a site of regional importance by P.T. Harding (1978). Attention is drawn to other specialist recorders below.

1. Insecta

Some groups of insects have been recorded more fully than others. The enormity of the task is apparent when it is realised that nearly 4,000 species of beetles and nearly 6,000 species of flies occur in Britain. The forty or so dragonflies are easy going by comparison.

i. *Orthoptera*: Five orthopterans have so far been recorded, but several further species are to be expected. The species recorded are *Chorthippus parallelus*, *C. brunneus*, *Omocestus viridulus*, *Meconema thalassinum* and *Leptophyes punctatissima*.

ii. *Odonata*: The damselflies and dragonflies have been recorded fairly thoroughly, and eleven species have been identified. Early summer is dominated by the damselflies *Enallagma cyathigerum* and *Ischnura elegans*, with fewer *Calopteryx splendens*, which are readily identified by the dark bar on their wings. The Red-eyed Damselfly (*Erythromma najas*) was first recorded in 1983: it is restricted to the water-lilies *Nuphar lutea* by the Grand Bridge. This species is known from only eight localities in Oxfordshire (Campbell, 1983). *Orthetrum cancellatum* and *Libellula depressa* are the first dragonflies to emerge. By mid-August the large dragonflies, *Aeshna cyanea*, *A. grandis*, *A. juncea* and *A. mixta* are on the wing. *Aeshna mixta* was first recorded in Blenheim in 1985. The small dragonfly *Sympetrum striolatum* is on the wing usually into late September.

Chelmick *et al.* (1980) state that in most parts of Britain any site with ten or more breeding species of *odonata* should be categorised as being of regional importance on the grounds of diversity. However, not all of the eleven species present have been proved actually to breed at Blenheim.

iii. *Hemiptera*: To date just over thirty species of heteroptera have been identified. They range from the widespread shield bugs such as *Sehirus bicolor* to the arboreal *Elasmucha grisea* and *Elasmostethus interstinctus*. *Myrmus miriformis*, which feeds especially on unripe grass seeds, occurs on the 'better' limestone grassland. Amongst the predatory bugs are such common species as *Dolichonabis limbatus* and *Himacerus apterus*. Mirid bugs so far identified include such common species as *Heterotoma planicornis* and *Harpocera thoracia*. Of a more specialised nature is *Monalcoris filicis*, which is restricted to Bracken (*Pteridium aquilinium*). A number of specialist oak-feeding species are to be expected.

In the Heteroptera collections of the Hope Department at the University Museum, Oxford, there are a number of water bugs collected by Dr. G.G.E. Scudder during August 1957. Nine species are represented in the collections, some of which are rare in Oxfordshire. The species are: *Microvelia reticulata*, *Cymatia coleoptrata*, *Callicorixa praeusta*, *Corixa dentipes*, *Gerris odontogaster*, *G. lacustris*, *G. argentatus*, *Notonecta glauca* and *N. marmorea*. In 1982 *Mesovelia furcata* was taken, apparently only the second record for Oxfordshire.

Only a few common species of homoptera have so far been identified. *Cercopis vulnerata* and *Cicadella viridis* are widespread in Oxfordshire, mostly in damper situations. *Jassus lanio* is found on the oaks and *Aphrophora alni* is present on most species of bushes and deciduous trees.

iv. *Megaloptera*: A few odd records of these insects have been made. The Snakefly, *Raphida cognata*, is present. The alderfly *Sialis lutaria* is often abundant along the margins of the lake. Much research still needs to be done on these insects.

v. *Lepidoptera*: To date 25 species of butterflies have been recorded, but several further species are almost certainly present. Of some note is the Essex Skipper, *Thymelicus lineola*, which is still very local in Oxfordshire. The Brown Argus, *Aricia agestis*, is found in association with the Rock Rose, *Helianthemum chamaecistus*, upon which its larvae feed. Both the Dingy Skipper, *Erynnis tages*, and the Grizzled Skipper, *Pyrgus malvae*, occur, but are generally not that common in Oxfordshire. The White-letter Hairstreak, *Strymonidia w-album*, has been recorded as recently as 1978, and probably survives in small numbers; it had been feared that this butterfly might become almost extinct through the ravages of Dutch Elm Disease, since its caterpillars feed upon the leaves of both the Common Elm, *Ulmus procera*, and the Wych Elm, *Ulmus glabra*; but there are still plenty of young shoots, particularly of the latter species, in the park, and it is assumed that the caterpillars feed quite happily on such growths.

Only a short list of moths compiled in the late 1970s by M. Crewe is in existence. Regular moth trapping in the ancient oak woodland should provide a lengthy and impressive list of moth species.

vi. *Coleoptera*: A little general collecting has taken place, and about one hundred different beetles have been recorded. D. Copestake recently took the rare cerambycid beetle *Grammoptera holomelina*. Amongst the other beetles is the carabid *Cychus rostratus*, which eats snails. R.W. Lloyd published a few records in the *Entomologists' Monthly Magazine* in 1954, but attention was only drawn to nationally rare species such as *Rhizophagous oblongicollis* and *Plectophleus rutidus*. Both of these species are category I in the Red Data Books. Angus (1965) has published a few records of the family *Histeridae* from Blenheim Park.

C. Johnson undertook some work on the fauna of the old oaks in 1978. Although his list is quite short, a number of notable species were recorded, including *Abaeus granulum*, *Aeletes atomarius* (both Red Data Book Category 3 species), and the rare *Anaspasis schilskyana*, *Pediacus dermestoides* and *Plagaderus dissectus*. That so many rare species should occur in such a comparatively short list does indicate the richness of the coleoptera fauna to be found in Blenheim Park.

vii. *Hymenoptera*: Hornets, *Vespa crabro*, are seen in most years; they are considered to be an indicator species of 'good' ancient woodland. The oaks show the deformed acorns caused by the gall wasp *Andricus quercus-calicis*. This species is a recent colonist of Oxfordshire, and indeed of Great Britain. Much work still needs to be done on this group of insects.

viii. *Diptera*: A few common species, mostly syrphids, have been identified. D.M. Ackland has collected *Anthomyiidae*, but as yet his lists are unavailable.

2. *Arachnida*

Johnson in 1978 found four species of pseudoscorpions, *Neobium muscorum*, *Roncus lubricus*, *Chthonius ischmocheles* and *Dendrochemes cyrneus*. Blenheim Park is one of only four sites in Britain where viable populations of the last species are known.

No records of spiders existed previously for Blenheim Park, so a little collecting has been undertaken by the present author and C. Hambler. C. Hambler has undertaken all the identifications, with the exception of *Erigonidium graminicola*, which was determined by Dr. P. Merrett. Some 40 species have been identified.

Several species are of note. *Zygiella stroemi* is considered to be nationally rare, being associated with the trunks of old Oak trees. In Blenheim it is associated with Oaks and also with the large Cedars. *Achaearanea simulans*, also a national rarity, also occurs; this is found in damp woodland. *Achaearanea tepidariorum* has been found in the butterfly house. This species needs warmth, and was formerly common in greenhouses, but the increasing use of pesticides has caused it to become far less frequent.

3. *Mollusca*

Goriup (1976) lists only ten species of freshwater molluscs, but more are undoubtedly present in the lakes. *Bithynia tentaculata* was the only species of note, being regarded as an indicator of good-quality water. Blenheim has long been known for the size of its Swan Mussels, *Anodonta anatina*. One specimen in the County Museum collections measures over 17cm in length.

Sixteen species of terrestrial gastropods have been identified, the only species of note being the Roman Snail, *Helix pomatia*, which appears to be restricted to areas of warm, rough calcareous grassland. Only eight sites for this, the largest British snail, are known in Oxfordshire.

4. *Other Invertebrates*

P.D. Goriup (1976) gives a short list of the aquatic fauna in the River Glyme and the Queen Pool. The leeches *Helobdella stagnalis* and *Erpobdella testacea* were recorded, and only one or two previous Oxfordshire records are given by Mann & Watson (1964).

5. *Vertebrates*

i. *Fish*: Blenheim is well-known for its large Pike, *Esox lucius*, and specimens can occasionally be seen basking in the shallows. They undoubtedly take a toll on young water birds. During early summer Tench, *Tinca tinca*, can be seen spawning in the shallows. Other species present include Rudd, *Scardinius erythrophthalmus*, Roach, *Rutilus rutilus*, and Perch, *Perca fluviatilus*.

ii. *Reptiles and Amphibians*: The Common Frog, *Rana temporaria*, Toad, *Bufo bufo*, and Common Newt, *Triturus vulgaris*, occur around the lakes. M. Smith (1951) gives details of the Great Crested Newts, *Triturus cristatus*, breeding in the ornamental ponds in the formal gardens. No recent information on this species is available.

The reptiles so far recorded are Common Lizard, *Lacerta vivipara*, Slow Worm, *Anguis fragilis*, and the Grass Snake, *Natrix natrix*.

iii.   *Birds*: Birds are the one group that have been well-documented, especially in the region of the Queen Pool. The woodland areas have not been regularly surveyed. Brucker & Campbell (1975) listed 164 species of birds recorded within or over the park, and at the time of writing, autumn 1985, the total number of species has increased to 183. In addition, a number of birds which are either feral or escapes have also occurred. During November 1983 a small party of bird-watchers identified 62 species of birds in one day, and a solitary observer in April 1976 identified 55 species in only three hours. This gives some idea of the rich bird life that can normally be found in the park.

As with all wildlife, the status of the various species does not remain static. It is proposed here to use Brucker & Campbell (1975) as a base line, and only to review the newly-recorded species and some notable changes in status.

During the hot, dry period in August 1976 the water-level of the Queen Pool dropped, to reveal large areas of mud. A number of passage waders dropped in to feed, including Knot, *Calidris canutus*, Spotted Redshank, *Tringa erythropus*, and Wood Sandpiper, *Tringa glareola*, which were all new species for Blenheim. Other waders recorded only once or twice before included Little Ringed Plover, *Charadrius dubius*, and Greenshank, *Tringa nebularia*. Two other waders have also been added to the Blenheim list, a Black-tailed Godwit, *Limosa limosa*, in May 1980, and a Grey Phalarope, *Phalaropus fulicarius* in September 1981.

Water-fowl present many problems, as so many escape from collections and some then become established in the wild. A drake Ring-necked Duck, *Aythya collaris*, in February 1979, was accepted as a genuine visitor from North America. Ruddy Duck, *Oxyura jamaicensis*, Mandarin, *Aix galericulata*, and Wood Duck, *Aix sponsa*, have all become established in feral populations and occur with increasing frequency. Firecrest, *Regulus ignicapillus*, Raven, *Corvus corax*, and Little Gull, *Larus minutus*, are all becoming more widespread in Britain, and have been recorded within the park. The remaining additions are Red-necked Grebe, *Podiceps griseigena*, Marsh Harrier, *Circus aeruginosus*, Goshawk, *Accipiter gentilis*, Red-footed Falcon, *Falco vespertinus*, Dipper, *Cinclus cinclus*, Hoopoe, *Upupa epops*, and Water Pipit, *Anthus s.spinoletta*.

Amongst the status changes the most striking has been that of the Canada Goose, *Branta canadensis*. In the autumn of 1975 the total was 'up to thirty', and in the autumn of 1985 a total of over four hundred has been counted. Only a few pairs breed each year. Gadwall, *Anas streperas*, breed annually, but the autumn influx, peaking at 66 in 1979, has not occurred since 1982, although the wintering, especially post-Christmas, numbers have increased. Wintering Cormorants, *Phalacrocorax carbo*, have increased considerably in Oxfordshire, and many more sightings have been reported from Blenheim. Up to 1975 there were only five records from the park, but between January 1976 and October 1985 there have been thirteen records.

During the 1950s large flocks of Teal, *Anas crecca*, Shoveler, *Anas clypeata*, and Wigeon, *Anas penelope*, normally appeared during the winter, as did a 'raft' of Dabchicks, *Taybaptus ruficollis*. The dredging of the lakes in the 1960s rendered conditions unsuitable for these birds, but slowly their numbers are building up again each year, with the exception of the Dabchick.

iv. *Mammals*: Some sixteen species of mammals have been recorded, but there are glaring gaps in our records: no shrews or bats have yet been recorded, for example, although there are records of some species for Woodstock, and one can feel confident that they will also occur within the park.

The mounds of earth thrown up by Moles, *Talpa europaea*, are often quite numerous, but the animal itself is rarely seen, as is the case with the mostly nocturnal Hedgehog, *Erinaceus europaeus*. The numbers of Rabbit, *Oryctolagus cuniculus*, vary, with myxamatosis sweeping through every two or three years when the population has built up. Occasionally black Rabbits occur as natural 'sports'. Water Voles, *Arvicola amphibius*, can be seen, especially where the River Glyme enters the park. Brown Rats, *Rattus norvegicus*, may also be seen by the water's edge throughout. The exact date when the Grey Squirrel, *Sciurus carolinensis*, first colonised Blenheim Park has not been discovered, but today this rodent is abundant.

Predatory mammals are present in small numbers. Stoat, *Mustela erminea*, and Weasel, *Mustela nivalis*, are supplemented by feral Mink, *Mustela vison*, from the River Evenlode. Foxes, *Vulpes vulpes*, are present, but there are no records of Badgers, *Meles meles*.

The park wall keeps out the larger deer, but the Muntjac, *Muntiacus reevesi*, is now quite numerous in the denser areas of woodland.

Acknowledgements

My sincere thanks go to Mr P. Hutton, the agent, and Mr D. Mundy, head keeper, for most generously allowing me access to the private regions of the park. I would also like to thank all those people mentioned in the text who have helped with identifications and with records.

Bibliography

ANGUS R.B. 1965: '*Aeletes atomarius* and other Histeridae from Blenheim Park, Oxon', *Entomologists' Monthly Magazine* 101. 17.

BOWEN H.J.M. 1980: 'A Lichen Flora of Berkshire, Buckinghamshire and Oxfordshire', *Lichenologist* 12.

BRUCKER J.W. & CAMPBELL J.M. 1975: *The Birds of Blenheim Park.*

CAMPBELL J.M. 1983: *An Atlas of Oxfordshire Dragonflies* (Oxfordshire Museums Occasional Paper No. 3).

CAMPBELL J.M. 1985: *An Atlas of Oxfordshire Ladybirds* (Oxfordshire Museums Occasional Paper No. 8).

CHELMICK D. *et al.* 1980: *The Conservation of Dragonflies.*

GORIUP P. 1976: *River Survey Reports.*

HARDING P. 1978: *The Invertebrate Fauna of the Mature Timber Habitat.*

JONES E.W. 1953: 'A Bryophyte Flora of Berkshire and Oxfordshire', *Transactions of the British Bryological Soc.* Vol. 2, pts 1, 2, 4.

LLOYD R.W. 1954: '*Plectophloeus nitidus* in Oxfordshire', *Entomologists' Monthly Magazine* 90. 189.

MANN K.H. & WATSON E.V. 1964: *A Key to the British Freshwater Leeches.*

MAVOR W. 1811: *New Description of Blenheim* (8th edn.).

ROSE F. 1976: 'Lichenological indicators of age and environmental continuity in Woodlands' in BROWN D.H. *et al.*: *Lichenology: Progress and Problems.*

SMITH M. 1951: *The British Amphibians and Reptiles.*

INDEX